Bound I Newfoundland

The log of a young seaman on board the *Matthew*

Chris LeGrow

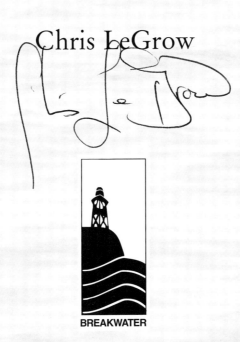

BREAKWATER

BREAKWATER

100 Water Street
P.O. Box 2188
St. John's, NF
A1C 6E6

BREAKWATER

Canadian Cataloguing in Publication Data

Legrow, Chris, 1976-

    Bound down for Newfoundland
    ISBN 1-55081-139-8 (hardcover) ; 1-55081-138-X (pbk)

1. Legrow, Chris, 1976- — Journeys — Newfoundland.
2. Matthew (Ship : Replica)   I. Title.

FC301.C3L44 1998   970.01'7'092   C98-950100-0
E129.C1L44 1998

Design and production: Nadine Osmond
Editing: Lara Maynard

Introduction

The sailor...

Never one to let an opportunity for adventure pass him by, Chris LeGrow could not resist the call of the sea and the magic of the *Matthew*. Ever so fittingly, Topsail, Newfoundland is where Chris calls home. But travel is a LeGrow family tradition (the surname is familiarly attached to a local travel agency), and Chris was on his way to Nepal in 1996 when he learned that applications for a spot on the crew of the replica of John Cabot's *Matthew* were being accepted. Many people would balk at the prospect of a seven week transatlantic voyage in a 20-metre square-sailed 15th century style caravel—or "tub," as Chris refers to the vessel in one of his candid personal log entries. With eight years of sailing experience already to his credit, Chris recognized a once-in-a-lifetime chance to put his seamanship to the test.

Chris began to compile his résumé of adventure early in life. His parents cultivated his predilection for travel with frequent family trips, and Chris has taken it from there with gusto. A friend provided his fateful introduction to small boat sailing. Together they took sailing lessons, raced competitively, and eventually placed second in the National Championship as members of Newfoundland and Labrador's Laser II sailing team in 1995. Chris circumnavigated the globe during 1994-1995 as a member of "Class Afloat" on the tall ship *Concordia*, completing Grade 13 in the process. He has since been sharing his enthusiasm for sailing as an instructor and coach for youths. And somewhere along the way, he has found the time and energy to sky-dive and climb two-thirds of the way to the top of the tallest peak in the world, Mount Everest!

And so at age 20, Chris was accepted as one of the youngest members of the 19-man crew of the *Matthew*—and a motley crew they were indeed, ranging in age up to 76 years and including doctors, journalists, and a clergyman, as well as professional seamen. These were constant companions for the long and sometimes trying trip across the broad Atlantic, sharing the challenge and excitement of retracing Cabot's historical trek from Bristol to Bonavista, and enduring its less glamorous aspects when the pomp subsided and the sea surrounded them. Whether the particular challenge of the day was facing galley duty to prepare the dreaded weekly serving of "chunky chicken," or seeing the ship through gales that stirred the sea into a frenzy, they were in it together, each one bringing his own skills to bear on the tasks at hand.

Chris shares the philosophy of motivational writer and speaker John Amatt, who realized a lifelong dream when he organized Canada's first successful expedition to complete the supreme climbing challenge of reaching the summit of Mount Everest in 1982. A profiler of Canadian adventurers, John encourages anyone who will listen to also push beyond their personal limitations and to embrace teamwork. He espouses the "adventure attitude," but his definition of adventure is an encompassing one. "Adventure isn't hanging on a rope on the side of a mountain," he says. "Adventure is an attitude that we must apply to the day-to-day obstacles of life—facing new challenges, seizing new opportunities, testing our resources against the unknown and, in the process, discovering our own unique potential."

Chris LeGrow's seagoing journal, reproduced here, is a record of the re-creation of an adventure into the unknown 500 years ago, an adventure which opened up all the possibilities of the New World to the people of Europe. It is simultaneously the record of Chris's personal adventure, documenting his bouts of homesickness, his moments of triumph, and his time alone in his thoughts afloat on the vast Atlantic, imbued with centuries of mariners' history. The log takes us along with Chris for the voyage while he sails, as his entry for May 20, 1997 closes, "Another hour, another watch, another day closer to home"—and closer to his next adventure.

...and the celebration

Naval architect Colin Mudie has said, "The *Matthew* was a bright new ship sailed by bright young men and I hope my replica reflects that." Mudie's replica, built at Redcliffe Quay, was the centrepiece of the cross-continental 1997 celebration of Italian explorer John Cabot's history making voyage from England to the New World in 1497. The ship and its would-be crew members, among them Newfoundland's Chris LeGrow, went through the rigors of sea trials and crew selection during the summer of 1996, sailing from England to Ireland and France. It was an eventful season plagued by mechanical problems and a serious accident for one sailor, but Chris pulled through with flying colours and received notice the following September that he would be among the crew that would guide the *Matthew* from Bristol to Newfoundland, where residents would be engaged in Cabot 500 Celebrations all year long.

On May 2, 1997 the *Matthew*'s crew and the ship's patron, Prince Philip, the Duke of Edinburgh, attended a service at Bristol Cathedral followed by a procession to the ship and blessing by the Lord Bishop of Bristol. Guests boarded the ship for the passage to the Cumberland Basin, with Prince Philip assisting the captain at the helm. The following day, when the *Matthew* passed through the lock into the Avon River for the third step of the voyage, was an exciting one marked by spectacles and sounds of celebration and the attendance of a throng of well-wishers. That evening the crew members were the guests of honour at a massive ball for 2000 people and then returned to the ship and moved across the harbour amidst fireworks and cannon fire. The pages of Chris LeGrow's log take the story from there and he tells it as only a member of the 1997 *Matthew* crew could.

Lara Maynard, Editor

May 3, 1997. Thousands of well-wishers flocked to the banks of the Avon River to witness the *Matthew* pass through the lock for the third step of the voyage.

Matthew Crew List

David Alan-Williams, Master

Terry Nash, Starboard Watch Captain

Russell Thiessen, Port Watch Captain

Chris LeGrow, Main Mast Hand Aloft

Nigel Church, Fore Deck Hand

Matthew Wills, Main Deck Hand

Martin Pick, Fore Deck Hand

Peter Zimonjic, Fore Mast Hand Aloft

Orlando Stuart, Main Deck Hand

John Jack Smith, Aft Deck Hand

Kevin O'Leary, Fore Mast Hand Aloft

Nick Craig, Main Mast Hand Aloft

Paul Venton, Fore Deck Hand

Mark Chislet, Main Deck Hand

Russell Owen, Chaplain

Stephen Greenwood, Main Deck Hand

James Roy, Bosun, Main Mast Hand Aloft

Gerry Gibbs, Main Deck Hand

Luke Porter, Main Deck Hand

The *Matthew*'s crew. Front, left to right: Orlando Stuart, Nick Craig, Paul Venton, Gerry Gibbs, Mark Chislet, Matthew Wills, Chris LeGrow. Back, left to right: Rev. Russell Owen, Kevin O'Leary, Steve Greenwood, Luke Porter, Terry Nash, David Alan-Williams, Russell Thiessen, James Roy, Peter Zimonjic, Nigel Church, John Jack Smith. Missing: Martin Pick.

Saturday, May 3, 1997

I awoke to the sounds of the city this morning, after spending the night hidden under the *foredeck armed with a *belaying pin to deter any locals thinking about securing a souvenir from the *Matthew*. It promised to be a beautiful day as I watched the rays of sun slowly creep across the deck. While the day started out peacefully, this quickly changed for me when I remembered what events were in store. The "big departure" from Bristol was set for the afternoon, which meant that we would spend the morning loading enough gear and food to last for seven weeks.

The readiness of the ship and crew weighed heavily on my mind, coupled with the stress of dealing with the media and promoters. The pressure was beginning to get to me, since I have never been involved in an event of this magnitude before. On top of that, I had a falling out with the captain last night and, as of this morning, I was uncertain about whether I would still make the voyage.

So I was a bundle of emotions this morning as I helped John Jack rig up a pulley which we would use to load the heavy crates of food onto the ship. While we worked John Jack helped me sort through my anxiety and regain my confidence, affirming the trust we have in each other. In a day's time I will have to trust the rest of the crew with my life.

Position: Bristol, Avon, England

Before the departure from Bristol. My favourite place aboard ship was up in the rigging because of the view it offered, as well as the quiet, and I missed being up there once the trip was over.

belaying pin: a pin in a ship's rail around which ropes can be fastened

foredeck: the part of a ship's main deck closest to the bow

Leaving Bristol on May 3, 1997. It was great to be finally underway, but the buildup of stress from all the festivities and contemplating the challenges that might be ahead made it the hardest day of the whole voyage.

Sunday, May 4, 1997

After participating in something akin to a Broadway production for the last couple of days, it was finally time to start the adventure. At 8:30 this morning we moved into the Bristol Channel, where the wind was whipping up steep chocolate-coloured waves. There was no turning back now.

People crowded the shoreline to wave farewell and an old paddle boat followed us out the channel. It was full of spectators who all rushed to the rail to get a picture as they passed alongside us, causing the boat to list badly in the heavy sea. I saw the mates and crew desperately trying to counteract the situation.

The wind and waves were directly on our nose, making the progress out of the channel challenging and slow. The conditions demanded the skills of an experienced seaman, so the skipper called upon John Jack to bring the *Matthew* *windward. While some of the crew were feeling the aftereffects of last night's farewell party combined with the steep sea, John Jack seemed not to miss a beat.

My first watch of the voyage was from 07:00 to 13:00 hours. I wasn't totally seasick, but I wasn't feeling altogether well, either. Halfway though the watch the captain told me to run up and set the *topsail, as a helicopter would be coming by in a few minutes to take promotional pictures for one of our sponsors. Heading up to the *crow's nest is not usually a problem for me, but I had not been to sea for a month and the conditions in the channel did not make for a pleasant reintroduction to life on the water. The roll on deck was not really bad, but the roll 70 feet up made going to the crow's nest a surefire way to become sick. Grumpily but carefully, I climbed up there to perform my first sailing duty of the voyage.

The *Matthew*'s topsail is mostly for show, but setting it requires patience and good balance. With only two hands to work one *halyard, two *sheets and two *braces, things can become a bit tangled. After about 10 minutes of struggling with the sail, my balance and my stomach, I was ready for the helicopter to arrive so that we could get this ordeal over with. "Another five minutes," the captain yelled from the deck. By this time I was sitting in the bottom of the crow's nest with hardly enough energy to yell back. Seasickness began to set in assuredly and I began to wonder where I could throw up. Not *leeward because it would land on the *mainsail and I'd have to face the task of cleaning it; not windward because it would blow back in my face; and not *astern because the captain and some of the crew were standing directly below.

After half an hour passed and there was still no sign of the helicopter, I called it quits and cautiously descended. It was the first time I was a little scared aloft. The nausea that had set in made me weak, slow and unbalanced, so it took me about five minutes to come down the rigging. As I sprawled across the deck I heard a noise—the helicopter.

Position: mouth of Avon River

Distance Run: 15 *nm

astern: aft; toward or at the rear of a ship

brace: a rope attached to the yard of a ship; it extends to the deck and is used to swing the yard when trimming the sails

crow's nest: a lookout platform near the top of the mast of a ship

halyard: a tackle or rope used to lower or raise a ship's flag, yard or sail

leeward: on the side away from the wind; or, in the direction toward which the wind is blowing

mainsail: the largest sail of a ship; it is located on the mainmast or principal mast of a ship

nm: nautical mile; a sea mile, the standard unit of nautical distance is the equivalent of 6 076.11549 feet

sheet: a rope attached to a corner of a sail which controls the angle at which the sail is set

topsail: a sail attached to a yard on a square-rigged ship's topmast

windward: on the side toward the wind; or, in the direction from which the wind is blowing

Changing a sail in Bristol.

Monday, May 5, 1997

Morning watch started at seven. We are all tired from the last week of festivities and some of the crew are seasick, homesick or lovesick after leaving behind wives, children, other family and friends. The departure from Bristol, down the Avon River, just two days ago was an event that I will never forget, with well over 100 000 people lining the banks of the river to watch us leave. Months of preparation had finally paid off, and not one of the crew was below the decks. Even Skipper was waving! There were cannons and firecrackers from the Avon Bridge and 100 000 people waving, screaming and cheering—a world record! I never stopped waving.

The people of Bristol really supported the *Matthew* and donated a lot of their time to its construction. It was hard to say goodbye to these people who have been so supportive of our voyage and treated the crew well.

Today is our first full day at sea and all the crew members are slowly getting used to life out here. Night watch has been cool and windy and the breeze is on our nose, prompting us to rely on the motor. That is unfortunate, as we are all sailors, but it allows us to power the stereo!

Russell Owen, our chaplain, was a little seasick last night and kept asking God why it was taking so long for His divine intervention. James, our *bosun, was hung-over and seasick—almost a permanent state for him. But the skipper has been in an upbeat and smiling mood since departure, which was rare before. The weight of pleasing Bristol is off his back now and pressure from Newfoundland hopefully won't be a problem until we are a couple of miles out.

As the day comes to an end, we have altered our plans and have changed course to a place called Milford Haven to ride out the gale which we have encountered. We damaged our propeller on the 3rd and it is interfering with the effectiveness of the engines.

It feels strange to look at the stars above tonight, 500 light years away, knowing that this is the same light that was produced as John Cabot began his voyage across the Atlantic. That same light is reaching our eyes now, more brilliant than ever. Bright stars and beautiful sunsets are some of the wonderful things about being at sea.

All's well!

Position: 51°24.3 N; 4°42.8 W

Wind Speed: 10-15 knots

Sea State: 3-5 m

Current: 3 knots

Speed (Average): 4-5 knots

Distance Run: 69.3 nm

Breakfast: bacon, eggs, bread, beans, raspberry drink
Lunch: curried chicken and rice (gross!), chocolate bar

bosun: boatswain; a ship's officer responsible for the rigging, anchors and ropes, and directing some of the work of the crew

Descending from the lock into the Avon River at Bristol, May 3, 1997. The Avon Suspension Bridge, where a million firecrackers hung, is visible in the background. As we passed under the bridge we fired our four canons in unison, the firecrackers exploded, and the *Concorde* soared overhead.

May 3, 1997. There was always a Newfoundland flag waving in the crowd of thousands of people at the *Matthew*'s departure from Bristol.

Tuesday, May 6, 1997

I am trying out different ways of writing this log so that it is easier to follow, so please bear with me.

At about 4:00 this morning we decided to quit trying to seek refuge from the gale at Milford Haven and headed for Ireland instead. We set sail with the wind from the northeast, until it banked around to the northwest, sending us on a course to the south. Even with all the high-tech gear on the ship, it still takes good, keen seamanship to sail her windward. The day was partly cloudy and cool, but the ship had become more stable with all of the sails set.

We had many visitors today. A fighter jet pilot did a couple of low passes and waved to us. A coastal fishery patrol plane came along half an hour later to do a couple of low passes and snap a few photos. We also caused the diversion of many cargo ships' courses, as they would come over to check us out.

Work continued as usual through the day, with more of the crew getting their sea legs. We learned that it wasn't 100 000 people who saw us leave on Saturday, but actually 500 000! But all of that is behind us and we all must concentrate hard on sailing the ship. The homesickness is slowly fading, but I am not over it yet. It is difficult to deal with and hard to control, but to be able to survive out here one must be able to understand it.

The engine is off and all we can hear is the wind and the waves beating against the hull. All we can see is the stars and the fluorescent bursts of green light from the plankton. I am lulled into sleep by the tranquility and my homesick thoughts are slowly replaced by dreams of adventure.

'Til tomorrow.

Position: 51°27.34 N; 5°30.17 W

Wind Speed: NWN 20 knots

Speed: 3-6 knots

Course: 295°mag.

Sea State: 1-2 m

Visibility: good

Sea Temp.: 7°C

Temp.: 100°C

Sails Set: *lateen, mainsail, *mainstay sail, *foresail, *spritsail

Distance Run: 40.6 nm

Breakfast: oatmeal, Harvest Crunch cereal, yogurt, juice, fruit
Lunch: mushroom soup, bread, apple
Supper: dehydrated chunky chicken, peas, mashed potatoes, and cheesecake for dessert

forecourse: foresail; the square sail attached to the lowest yard of a ship's forward mast

lateen sail: a triangular sail on a short mast which is held up by a long yard

mainstay: a rope or wire supporting the mainmast of a ship and extending to the bow

spritsail: a foot-and-aft sail supported by a sprit

Wednesday, May 7, 1997

Today was much like yesterday: sunny, cool, rough and windy. The wind was steady from the northeast until the afternoon when it shifted to the northwest and increased in strength. Right now it is blowing about 40 knots and some waves are reaching 20 feet. The rough weather has made it difficult for the crew to get any real work accomplished. There is a lot to be done with the *rigging, but the line needed to do the work is stuck in the *bilge. Most of the coils had to be stored there in order to save space, but so much is packed in there that now we cannot get it out. After three hours of trying to get some line, Mark and I were ready to break out the chainsaw and do some cutting. At least I was able to finish making up the *ratlines and do a bit of *tallowing.

The wind always seems to be against us. We are all having a hell of a time trying to go windward. The design of the vessel, coupled with most of the crew's lack of experience sailing a medieval style ship, makes it difficult for us to get anywhere. It will be a personal challenge for me and for the rest of the guys to be able to effectively steer the ship on course by the time we reach Bonavista. But I guess that it is all a part of the adventure. Cabot is either laughing at us or crying because there might only be one or two little things that we are doing wrong which could make all the difference if they were better handled.

I have *galley duty tomorrow and I am not looking forward to it. I don't mind the rough weather, but trying to cook in it will be havoc. I am sure that I'll have lots to say about it tomorrow.

I got an email today from Mom. My family returned safely from Bristol to Newfoundland, but a friend of the family is sick.

The only real company we have out here now are the seagulls that gracefully follow the ship for scraps. We are in our own little world.

Position: 50°52.6 N; 6°43.7 W

Wind Speed: 15-20 WNW

Speed: 3-5 knots

Course: 260°

Sea State: 3-5 m

Visibility: 5 miles

Sea Temp.: 11.5°C

Temp.: 5-10°C

Sails Set: all; mainsail closed 5:00 p.m. (17:00)

Distance Run: 79.7 nm

bilge: the lowest part of the hold of a ship; also the bottom of the hull of a ship

galley: a ship's kitchen

ratlines: small ropes that cross the shrouds of a ship; they are used for going aloft

rigging: the chains, cables and ropes used to work and support a ship's masts, sails and yards

tallow: to coat with a greasy substance

Thursday, May 8, 1997

The table that I write on tonight shakes violently beneath me. We have *struck all of the sails and are now heading due west, into the wind for Ireland. It has been quite discouraging to most of the crew to have the wind at our noses 95 percent of the time. The design of the *Matthew*'s sails allows us only to sail with the wind at our beam, so we cannot make any headway upwind. We are doing a bit better than we were before, but we still often wonder how Cabot did it. The wind is expected to be like this the entire journey. If it is, we'll all be crazy by the time we reach Bonavista. Either Cabot sailed during an exceptional year when the wind blew from the east to windward or he was just really good!

I am tired after my first full galley day with Doc Nick. It stared off badly with things flying everywhere with the roll of the ship, but we slowly got used to it and by dinner we were zooming around like pros. I made a pretty mean cheesecake and 10 buns. The dehydrated food is fairly easy to cook and tastes pretty good when fresh vegetables are added. Most of the food supplies on board are powdered or pre-made, just-add-water items which save space and are easily prepared—luckily for me! The menus are the same for each day of the week, so we'll have the same thing seven times.

Sunday is medieval day with medieval food, music, dress and attitude! We'll have a crew dinner and will be allowed one beer each, the highlight of the week.

There were many notable occurrences today. A line squall came through at about noon and snapped the mainstay sail halyard belaying pin in two. That caused the sail to drop in the water and act like a brake. It was in danger of catching in one of the props, but the guys managed to get it in and reset it. Then about mid-afternoon we had a visit from a pod of dolphins. Seven or eight of them played around the bow for a couple of hours, interrupting the crew's work. How often do we get to watch dolphins, though?

I got the night off from night watch because of the galley day. I am looking forward to a good night's sleep and a day of hard work tomorrow. We hope to be in Ireland by Saturday or Sunday.

Oh no! James and Mark are cooking tomorrow! We are all going to starve!

Position (Noon): 51°21.6 N; 6°28.9 W

Wind Speed: NWN 10-15 knots

Speed: 3-5 knots

Course: 340°

Sea State: moderate

Visibility: good

Sea Temp.: 11°C

Temp.: 5-10°C

Sails Set: struck all sails; motor

Distance Run: 8.1 nm

struck: lowered

Friday, May 9, 1997

It has been six days since we've been at sea and today was definitely the best. For most of the crew the shower that we had today was our first in over a week. The water wasn't hot or highly pressurized, but it got us clean, which is all that matters. Together with the good night's sleep I had, the shower made me feel refreshed and eager to work on the rigging.

I spent today with Russell Owen *tarring the main shrouds. It's a messy job, but it protects the natural hemp from decay caused by the salt water and sun. I also added a new knot to my collection—a *manrope knot. It is a stopper knot which I will use in my new belt.

The wind finally took a change for the better and backed around to southwest-west. This allowed us to steer an almost direct course to our target. It was a great welcome after days of forcing the ship to sail upwind.

Everything else seems to be fine. The email is up and running and many of the guys are receiving their first messages from home. All the ship's systems are working fine except for the bilge water level alarm which goes off whenever we hit a large wave. The alarm is designed to sound whenever the water in the bilge gets too high, but the rolling and splashing of the water sets it off all too often. It's especially loud and annoying when we are trying to get some sleep.

We should make our first stop in Ireland tomorrow at Crosshaven, where divers will inspect our damaged propeller. We will spend only a day there, then head to Bantry Bay for repairs.

I can't wait to phone home and have a pint!

Position (Noon): 51°31.6 N; 6°52.8 W

Wind Speed: 15-20 W

Speed: 4-5 knots

Course: 215°

Sea State: 3-5 m

Visibility: good

Sea Temp.: 11°C

Temp.: 9°C

Sails Set: *forestay sail, mainstay sail, lateen

Distance Run: 66.7 nm

forestay: a cable or rope extending from a ship's foremast to its bowsprit

forestay sail: the first sail in front of a ship's forward mast; it is a triangular sail attached to the forestay

manrope: a rope used as a handrail at the side of a ship's ladder or gangway

tar: to cover with tar; a ship's masts may be tarred to prevent the wood from rotting

Saturday, May 10, 1997

Today we arrived in a small Irish town called Crosshaven. It is a tiny fishing port and home to the Royal Cork Yacht Club, the oldest in the world. It was a task just to get into the harbour mouth. It took us two attempts against a strong head wind and swell to get around the headland which blocks the entrance. I was on the *helm for five and a half hours before we finally tied up. The area that we tied up in resembled a small Newfoundland fishing outport and the skipper had a hard job of getting the *Matthew* in between fishing trawlers and yachts.

As we were approaching the harbour earlier in the day we were forced to strike the aft-most sail, the lateen. This sail is always a handful to maneuver, and taking it down is no easy task. Before we had a chance to lash it down this time, the *half-ton spar rolled toward the mast, cracking off the *starboard prop throttle in the process. The skipper decided to use two throttles to maneuver into port, since doing that is more effective than using the rudder. This necessitated Mark using the throttle which is located beneath the *poop deck, from where he could not see anything. In order to coordinate the effort, I would shout to Mark to move the tiller right or left while the skipper called to him for prop power. The poor guy needed four hands to do the job, but all worked out well and we slipped in at about 17:30 to a small crowd of locals.

I then went off to find the only phone booth in town to call home and cure some of the homesickness I had been battling. All was well at home and it was good to hear everyone's voice.

The gang then headed off to a local pub called Cornin's, where the *Matthew*'s owner, Mike Slade, kindly picked up the tab. After a few pints, we headed back to the ship for a good night's sleep.

There is a lot of work to be done tomorrow— the sort of tasks that cannot be done at sea.

Position: 51°46.49 N; 8°02.52 W

Wind Speed: WSW 15-20 knots

Speed: 1-2 knots

Course: 260°

Sea State: 2 m

Visibility: good

Sea Temp.: 12°C

Temp.: 12°C

Sails Set: foresail, mainstay sail, lateen

Distance Run: 711 nm

half-ton spar: a stout pole used to support a ship's vessel

helm: the wheel or handle used to steer a ship

poop deck: the deck at the stern of the ship; it often forms the cabin's roof

starboard: the right side of a ship when facing forward

Sunday, May 11, 1997

A lot of work was done today, but there's not much to talk about. I finished the ratlines for the *shrouds in a couple of hours. It should be a bit easier to get into the crow's nest now.

The public visited the ship all day and I met a lady from Chicago whose husband is a Newfoundlander. Some of the other crew members and I went to the Cork Yacht Club in the evening. It is a nice place, but I thought it small for the oldest in the world. The sail school setup was quite nice. They must be getting ready for this year's Laser II World Championships.

A tasty dinner of pork and potatoes was prepared by our P. R. guy, David Redfern. I stuffed myself and then went for a beer at the yacht club. I'm tired now and am going to bed!

Position: Crosshaven, Ireland
Distance Run: 71.1 nm

South Coast of Ireland

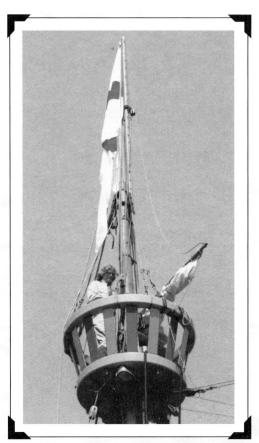

In the *Matthew*'s crow's nest.

shrouds: a series of ropes that help support a ship's mast

Monday, May 12, 1997

Today we head off for Castletownbere and some new propellers. It was a rough start and we almost ran ashore as we were leaving the channel. The wind was blowing right from the southwest, into the channel, and with our damaged props we had poor maneuverability. The swell and current caused us to drift toward shore and Skipper had to bear away and come around on the other *tack in order to avoid running aground. As he eased around, the wind pushed against the high stern of the *Matthew*, preventing us from going on the other tack. We were heading toward shore at 5 knots. We got the anchor ready to go, but luckily the ship came around just in time and we staggered out the channel. It was a hair-raising experience for a lot of us. We soon set sail and headed south and then tacked back towards land, trying to make progress into the wind. I am sure that they won't show that on television!

Our watch got stuck with the first shift of the day. We were all tired by then and the day seemed to go slowly.

It was great to talk to my family on the phone. I miss everyone more and more every day. I think that homesickness is one of the worst sicknesses of all because it attacks you when you're alone with your thoughts and causes a gut-wrenching feeling that is hard to describe. The only way to bear it is through mind power, so I try to concentrate on positive things.

It is getting close to the end of watch—sleep, finally!

Position: 51°47.31 N; 8°15.6 W

Wind Speed: SW 18-20 knots

Speed: 3 knots

Course: 177°

Sea State: moderate/rough

Visibility: bright

Sea Temp.: 11°C

Temp.: 10°C

Sails Set: forestay sail, mainstay sail, lateen

tack: a zigzag course against the wind; or, the direction of a ship's movement in regard to the position of its sails and wind direction

Tuesday, May 13, 1997

Today was beautiful and warm and a lot was accomplished. I finished our two new toilet rolls for the *heads. I used an old broom handle and lots of twine to jazz it up a bit. It was a small but important rigging job for the ship!

With the main and forestay sails set, we lumbered along to Castletownbere. The Irish coastline is brilliant with its rolling green hills, many lighthouses and homes. Near the end of night watch we passed the famous Fastnet Rock which is used as a marker in a big offshore sailing race held annually in the UK. It is to sailing here what the Montreal Forum is to Canadian hockey.

I got an email message from Dad today. It was all good. He even included the hockey scores, which were most appreciated.

Position: 51°27.8 N; 8°46.8 W

Wind Speed: WSW 5-10

Speed: 2 knots

Course: 265 °

Sea State: flat

Visibility: bright

Sea Temp.: 12°C

Temp.: 15°C

Sails Set: forestay sail, mainstay sail, lateen; engine

Distance Run: 72.0 nm

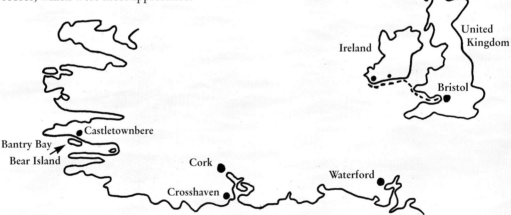

South Coast of Ireland

head: the lavatory of a ship

The *Matthew* entering Castletownbere for repairs. The coast of Ireland is magical and reminded me of home.

Wednesday, May 14, 1997

The entire coastline of Ireland happily reminds me of home as we round a point and enter Bantry Bay. We were followed by a large cruise ship at 6 a.m., but its crew had only a quick interest and didn't hassle us for long. With about 10 knots of breeze, Terry said that we are going too fast at 1 knot. It was one of the most insane things I've heard the whole trip. We have to wait for the tide to bring us into Castletownbere, a fishing port at the head of the bay.

We gave the square sails a nice furl and began to enter the harbour at around 7 a.m., when we were supposed to get off watch, which had started at 4 a.m.. But our watch got the short end of the stick again and we had to stay up on deck. We ended up not getting any sleep all day and I finally turned in at 11:30 p.m..

We cast our lines at the main fishing pier, only to be moved across the harbour an hour later to get ready to slip out. In that time I had a chance to admire the natural beauty of the area. The harbour is surrounded by barren hills and there is a large island at its mouth called Bear Island. It reminded me of the barren land behind our family's cabin near Carbonear.

The ship-out process took forever. We first had to maneuver the ship in backwards over a lift, which was no small task, and then let the slow process of raising begin. As soon as she was resting her blocks, we broke out the paint and coated all the scratches on the underside from where we went aground in Bristol. Russell Thiessen and Terry installed the new propeller blades.

We all finished work at about 5:00 and headed over to the local hotel for a shower in one of its rooms. It gave me the chance to read, write and catch up on the news. A good pint at a historic pub called McCarthy's made the day all worthwhile.

Position: 51°38.6 N; 9°54.6 W

Wind Speed: 9 knots

Speed: 1.5 knots

Course: 335°

Sea State: flat

Visibility: 5 mile horizon

Sea Temp.: 11°C

Temp.: 5°C

Sails Set: motoring to port with lateen up

Distance Run: 71 nm

May 14, 1997. The *Matthew* was fitted with new propellers and got a fresh coat of paint at Castletownbere, County Cork, Ireland.

A final shot of the crew in medieval costume before departing from Ireland. Front: Mark Chislet, Kevin O'Leary, Terry Nash, Orlando Stuart. Second row: Paul Venton, Rev. Russell Owen, Nick Craig, David Alan-Williams, Steve Greenwood, Gerry Gibbs. Back: Russell Thiessen, Chris LeGrow, Luke Porter, Matthew Wills, Peter Zimonjic, Martin Pick, Nigel Church, John Jack Smith. Missing: James Roy.

Kevin O'Leary and I with the coast of Ireland, the last land that we would see until the *Matthew* arrived in Bonavista, in the background.

Thursday, May 15, 1997

Position: on slip at Castletownbere, County Cork, Ireland

Friday, May 16, 1997

Today was the real thing. Without the pomp of Bristol, although with some difficulty, we slipped away from Castletownbere's fishing pier to start the five and a half week journey. There was only a small crowd there to see us off, compared to the 500 000 in Bristol. Some kids from a local school showed up, some townspeople and the *Matthew* support team.

Officially, the *Matthew* is ready to get underway. Then why do I feel so weird? The ship is solidly built and designed well. I think that this little beauty can stand up to anything the Atlantic decides to throw at her. So why do I lie in my bunk at night or sit on the shore, watching the ship glow, and feel so doubtful?

I am not an expert seaman or team builder, but I've been on various teams in my life and I know what the bond feels like with everyone knowing each other's abilities. There is a core group of sailors on this ship who are going to have a lot of responsibility on their hands. I feel scared, because who is going to be there to back up that group of sailors when they get tired? Lots of things can happen at sea. Storms are loud and confusing and one can very easily become disoriented. Only through experience can one do the job safely and efficiently. A person without experience is a risk to the ship, to himself and to the crew. A third of the crew have that needed experience, and only half of it on a tall ship.

I don't usually cry when saying goodbye to my family. But today on the dock, all alone in a phone booth, I said goodbye to my parents and cried. The only way I can explain the voyage in front of me is by comparing it to another kind of challenge, mountain climbing. Right now I feel like a climber who is half way up a mountain, reaching for the summit, the goal. Yet it lays covered in a cloud of mystery. As we left today, and even now on my first night watch, such a cloud lays thick around us and I wonder what challenges and rewards lie ahead. At least the wind is cooperating, blowing on our quarter as we head northwest.

This experience is really testing my limits. I have jumped out of planes with confidence that the parachute on my back would do its job. But it is hard to feel totally safe when crossing the Atlantic during the worst part of the year on a small medieval style ship. I have committed myself to this adventure, far from the safety net of home, and have prepared for the trip for months, doing everything from getting the right clothes and equipment to rigging and making the ship safe. Yet it seems that nothing can be done to subside the fear I feel. But one must face one's fears in the face, they say, though I wonder at what cost. Did Cabot and his men experience this sort of fear and excitement mingled? I remind myself that there is nothing more rewarding than taking a risk and having a successful outcome.

I write this log now as we move slowly out through the icy Atlantic. A stray swallow has landed upon the ship and is now resting on the poop deck. I do not know if that's a good or bad sign, but it is a beautiful creature and I guess it does not matter.

My thoughts are clustered as I try to sort out what direction my mind should take. My watch leader, our "responsible head," lays sleeping in the navigation room, missing the log entry again while the rest of us are on deck in the cold. We are tired too, but someone has to sail the ship home.

Strange things, very strange things. My mind has wings.

Position: 51°37.0 N; 9°55.57 W
Wind Speed: SE 18 knots
Speed: 5 knots!!!
Course: 270°
Sea State: 1-2 m
Visibility: overcast
Sea Temp.: 11°C
Temp.: 10°C
Sails Set: sprit, foresail, mainsail, lateen—full sail!!
Distance Run: 10 nm

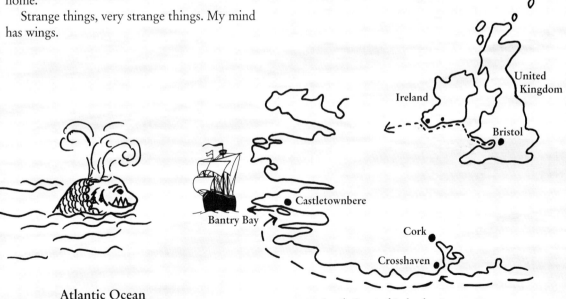

Atlantic Ocean

South Coast of Ireland

Saturday, May 17, 1997

The Atlantic has grown calm today, leaving us to drift slowly in its fog-kissed swells. It is like being stuck in the *doldrums without the warm weather. Last night's watch proved to be the most boring yet. It was the first time during the voyage that we were sailing with the wind, so things were smooth and the wind wasn't as bone-frosting. Mark, still hung-over from the night before, took the opportunity to sleep during watch (No! No!). He did it standing up against the poop deck rail. The roll of the boat was smooth, so he was able to stay upright—until a freak wave came along and sent him flying to a rude awakening. It was quite amusing!

Today was another galley day for Nick and I. The meals for the next two weeks will be pretty good. We have a lot of fresh food to eat before it goes bad. We had a big fry-up for breakfast: bacon, eggs, potatoes and sausages.

The weather has been perfect so far, but we had our first breakdown of the trip only a day out. The starter for the engine burnt out somehow, and we didn't have any replacement parts.

This was not a good situation. Our batteries were running low, I had food to cook, and we also had to navigate. I was a little concerned because of our position relative to the shore. We were no more than 10 miles off land and if the wind unexpectedly turned west, as it is known to do, we would have had a first class ticket back to Ireland. Skipper used our satellite phone to call back to the office and arranged for a fishing boat to bring out the spare part. Money talks.

It is funny how most of the gear on board made to 15th century standards is holding up better than our expensive 21st century gear. Technology always causes hassles, especially in the middle of the ocean.

Russell Thiessen, our engineer, managed to *jury-rig another starter and she was up and running like a song. I never thought I would like the sound of that loud engine in my ear as I sleep, but it was a great relief to hear it.

After that incident, Kevin had a little accident aloft when he dropped a bucket of tar all over the sail and deck. Needless to say, I was not impressed. That is my sail he dumped on and tar is a tough thing to clean up.

We just received news that the fishing boat will be late arriving. I am on the 3 a.m. night watch now and we are all below, lazing around and reading month-old magazines.

The galley that Nick and I did turned out fine, with a great spaghetti sauce with dinner, followed by cheesecake. The cleanup took longer than expected, but we got to listen to some great tunes all the same.

doldrums: ocean regions near the equator where the wind is weak or shifts constantly; sailing ships in doldrums have difficulty making any headway

jury-rig: a temporary rig on a ship

Position: 52°12.2 N; 11°07.2 W
Wind Speed: SE 9 knots
Speed: 1-2 knots
Course: 330°
Sea State: flat, calm
Visibility: poor
Sea Temp.: 12.8°C
Temp.: 9°C
Sails Set: full sail
Distance Run: 73.1 nm

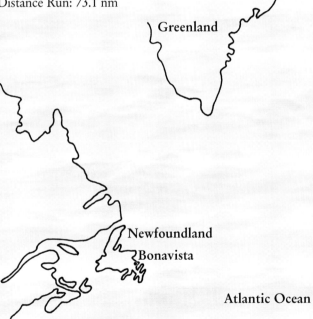

Greenland

Iceland

United
Kingdom

Newfoundland
Bonavista

Ireland

Bristol

Atlantic Ocean

Sunday, May 18, 1997

Medieval Sunday aboard could not have happened on a more beautiful day. It was more like a cruise ship atmosphere, with the off-watch group laying around the deck catching some rays. The wind was flat and the sun was hot. Some of us took the opportunity to wash and dry some clothes. There's nothing better than clean-smelling underwear!

At around 6 a.m. the shore team of David, Laurel and Ron arrived on the diving boat *Merlin Diver* with two new starter kits and some fresh bread. They stayed for a while, sipping on the keg of brandy that was given to the ship. After a good chat and the excitement of seeing the first whale of the voyage (a minke), they headed back off into the fog out of which they had earlier materialized. With that, the clouds parted, the wind came up a little, the sky appeared and Russell got to work on the new starter engine.

Unfortunately, the mechanical work was being done next to my bunk, so the amount of sleep I was supposed to get this morning was cut in half by constant swearing and talking. They got it set up and humming away, though. Good work!

Some of the other crew members and I are finding that dreams and nightmares have been more common in our sleep than they usually are. I tend to dream about the weirdest things which have no apparent relevance to sailing. I don't know if it is the movement of the ship that causes these dreams, but it ruins any sleep pattern that I have, making me vulnerable to migraine headaches.

Deck work was slow, but a few things were accomplished. We are trying to get some tasks done before bad weather hits, looking out for chafing and touching up paintwork.

Today was also a sad day for everyone aboard. A small swallow, lost at sea, came to the ship in the early morning to rest. He was quite tired and thirsty. We gave him some water to try to give him enough strength to fly back to land. Alas, he died in my hands. We wrapped him in a cloth with a weight tied to the bottom and Rev. Russell performed a little ceremony. It was short, but sweet, and we dropped the swallow into his watery grave just as the sun set. Although he didn't have a name, his determination to stay alive on his long journey from Africa will be remembered for the rest of the trip.

Position: 52°21.6 N; 11°23.8 W

Wind Speed: 7 knots south

Speed: 1.0 knot

Course: 310°

Sea State: calm

Visibility: bright

Sea Temp.: 11°C

Temp.: 15°C

Sails Set: full sail for about half the day

Distance Run: 5.3 nm (slow!)

May 18, 1997. A swallow that had been blown off course landed on the ship. It was very weak so Martin Pick fed it water in the hope that it would regain its strength, but it died in my wool hat later that evening.

A homing pigeon that had become lost during a storm spent a sunny day with us before taking off into the horizon.

Monday, May 19, 1997

The day started off with the starboard watch still tired from the sail maneuvers that occurred on the watch before. My watch raised and lowered all *yards twice, til finally they stayed lowered to reduce the roll of the ship. The only break came when the quiet of the night was suddenly broken by the soft sound of dolphins surfacing and playing on the bow wave. The moon was bright and we could see the trail of fluorescence which the dolphins left behind as they passed through the water. It was truly a memorable sight.

We are only half a week into the voyage, but a lot of the guys seem tired already. We worked really hard to get the ship ready before we left and none of us had time to get some rest. I figure that once we all fall into a routine after the first week, things will not be as tiring.

We did little things with the rigging today to prevent chafing and to maximize efficiency. We moved the anchor line on the lateen *brailing system more *aft so that it gathered more sail when engaged. We also moved the *clew lift block back behind the yard to improve that system. I tightened the para-tackle on the main yard so that it will not swing side to side as much when close to the deck. I also beefed up my knife holder a bit with a few fancy knots.

The sea is still relatively calm, but the temperature has dropped as a system slowly moves over us. It is a bit discouraging with the wind on our nose and motoring, but the forecast is for a storm with winds from the east. It has almost been too long for the sea to be so laid back. It has been nice, but I didn't try out for this voyage for a summer cruise across.

Position: 52°52.9 N; 13°02.2 W

Wind Speed: NW 6 knots

Speed: 1.0 knot

Course: 310°

Sea State: calm and swell

Visibility: overcast

Sea Temp.: 11°C

Temp.: 10°C

Sails Set: none; engine

Distance Run: 76.9 nm

aft: at or near the stern of a ship

brail: a small rope used in drawing a sail in or up

clew: a corner on a square sail or fore-and-aft sail; or a metal ring fastened on such a corner to allow the attachment of lines

yard: a long, slender beam or pole fastened across a mast and used to support a sail

Australian teacher Nigel Church, our fore deck hand.

One of the many sail maneuvers of the voyage. I am replacing a chafed line while trying to avoid being swung around by the rolling of the ship—no easy task!

Tuesday, May 20, 1997

We are still hanging around 160 miles off the Irish coast between two lows. The one that is approaching from the west will bring our first storm. If we get north of it enough, it will give us northeasterlies up to 50 knots—quite windy. So far, the trip from Ireland has been a walk in the park. The calm weather has allowed us to complete a lot of work, from finding and sealing leaks and working on the engine, to rigging up in the crow's nest, but the skill and strength of the crew will be determined over the next couple of days.

Not much out of the ordinary occurred today. Russell Owen keeps complaining that he has more hair on his face than on his head, and the crew tackled chunky chicken night. Chunky chicken is by far the worst of all the pre-prepared food on board. No matter what one adds to it, that spongy chicken flavour always seems to come through. The mashed potatoes and peas sometimes make it tasty, though it is still pasty. But it is all we have to eat and I am so hungry at the end of the day that I don't care if all the juice has been sucked out of the chicken!

Tonight we sail northwest by the bright moonlight that shimmers across the water. Another hour, another watch, another day closer to home!

Position: 53°27.15 N; 14°29.56 W

Wind Speed: NNW 13.0 knots

Speed: 20 knots

Course: 300°

Sea State: slight

Visibility: overcast

Sea Temp.: 11°C

Temp.: 14°C

Sails Set: none; engine

Distance Run: 59 nm

Hanging out on the bowsprit.

Wednesday, May 21, 1997

Having just witnessed a beautiful and inspiring sunset, words are useless to describe the emotions that flow through me at this very moment. After supper we set full sail as the wind shifted and rose from the southeast. The course we are taking has us basically sailing off into the sunset. The cloud colour was magnificent and the moonlight that shines on us now is just as beautiful. The engine has been shut off, and all one can hear is the creaking and the water hitting the side of the ship.

I sent my first email message today, half of which contained the usual "hi's" and "I love you's," and the other half a request to my Dad to shorten his emails to a page or two. The captain doesn't like it when we get long messages because it costs per character to send them by satellite.

Dad likes to write informative email, but when he starts giving me reports on the weather in Calgary it has to stop. Also, the whole point of going to sea is to get away from all of that.

Somehow on the *Matthew* technology never seems to leave us alone. But I still do not mind the emails.

Time to sign off. The first *Nimrod* pass is tomorrow and everyone on board is excited about that. I'll write more on the details of that procedure tomorrow.

Position: 53°56.57 N; 15°27.8 W
Wind Speed: 8-9 knots SE at 16:00 hrs.
Speed: 1-2.5 knots
Course: 330°
Sea State: 1-3 m; moderate; ship rolling heavily at times
Visibility: clear, partly cloudy
Sea Temp.: 13.1°C
Temp.: 14°C
Sails Set: full sail at 19:00 hrs.
Distance Run: 55.4 nm

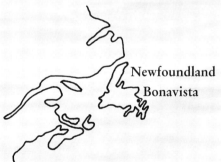

Atlantic Ocean

Thursday, May 22, 1997

Another fast-tracking day on the North Atlantic. We are doing 5.5 nautical miles an hour—not a bad average. The swell has become much larger, making life on board a little more difficult.

We all know when a new helmsman is taking a shift because the boat starts to roll a lot more as that person tries to get accustomed to the sensation of steering. It is a little frustrating when the ship is not driven correctly. Two-thirds of the guys haven't helmed a vessel of this size before, so they are not used to the characteristics that she has. Granted, the *Matthew* is a difficult ship to sail, but a lot of pressure has landed on the more experienced crew members to teach those other guys the ropes and then to sail as best they can themselves to make up for lost distance.

Sail settings and sail shape are also gray areas, even amongst the watch captains and to the skipper. We are constantly trimming sails and checking for chafe in the rigging. Hopefully everyone's skill levels will pick up soon with the hands-on experience.

It has almost been a week since we left Ireland and we are slowly running out of fresh food. We are using up everything before the "best before" dates. Soon we will be into powdered and canned food—yummy.

We had our first *Nimrod* pass today. All the video taken in the last week was successfully beamed up, which took about two hours. Steve and Orlando got some footage over the last week with wonderful sunsets and great sailing. They also have footage of a watch change at 03:00.

Needless to say, we were not thrilled to be filmed during that sleepy transition. Most of us do not look like we are alive as we stumble on deck. Before it left, the *Nimrod* did a couple of very fast low level passes, shaking the ship as it went by.

We ate well today, with Kevin "The Cook" cooking up a storm. I spent most of the day watch honing my skill at the helm. At one point we reached 7 knots! No record breaker, but not bad for a tub.

I sign off now as we roll violently in the merciless swell. The moon is out in full beam tonight, disappearing amongst the clouds periodically, blackening our view of the ocean. The seabirds continue to play in the warm updraft created by the wind moving around the sails. They never stop!

Position: 54°54.28 N; 17°03.7 W

Wind Speed: ESE 22.0 knots!!!

Speed: 5-7.0 knots!!!

Course: 330°

Sea State: moderate

Visibility: sunny

Sea Temp.: 12°C

Temp.: 10°C

Sails Set: full sail; rolling and billowing

Distance Run: 83.9 nm

The *Matthew* at her best, cutting through the Atlantic in full sail. We actually sailed for 90 percent of the trip and barely relied on our motor.

Friday, May 23, 1997

It has been a week since we left Bantry Bay and almost a month til we'll be in Bonavista. It was another unusual day in the Atlantic, relatively warm and partly sunny. We had the morning watch, which was the only part of the day that had sun. With the layers of clothes slowly peeled off and bare feet, I helmed the ship for about four hours. The wind was fresh from the southeast with a cross swell from the south that created a substantial roll.

The BBC did some filming from the crow's nest with Paul. They wanted to film someone who rarely ventures high. It was funny to watch because the bad cross swell caused havoc near the top. He did it, though, and we were all happy for him.

For many of us it was the day to take off week one's clothes and open up week two's. Unfortunately, some of the crew discovered that it had gotten soaked by the leak we had in the main hatch a couple of days ago. By afternoon the ship looked like a Chinese laundry, with clothes hanging from everywhere possible.

It was also another busy day for wildlife. Another lost swallow decided to make the ship its last resting place. I felt like the swallow grim reaper. We also had a sighting of a pod of about 50 whales off in the distance. It was the first time that many of the crew members saw more than one whale at a time. We also had a sucker fish attached to the rudder, but Terry and the skipper managed to remove the underwater hitchhiker with a pole.

A lot of the crew are finding it hard to sleep in the evenings and are tired. The severe rolling seems to have an effect on people's sleeping patterns. Couple that with the loud creaking of the ship, and one tends to find it hard to concentrate. I am sure that we will all be used to the odd sleeping patterns when we finally leave. We will all still be getting up at three o'clock to do night watch!

Another beautiful day, another day without a shower! My hair has decided to form its own style and shape. The areas of dried tar have helped me to hold the hair back from my face. Little dreadlocks are popping up everywhere, making me look like someone from Jamaica. At least I do not smell—I think!

Position: 54°30.6 N; 19°53.1 W

Wind Speed: 11-14 knots; SW/SE

Speed: 3-5 knots

Course: west, 260-280°

Sea State: light-moderate; bad cross swell

Visibility: excellent

Sea Temp.: 13.7°C

Temp.: 12°C

Sails Set: full sail, set for a broad reach

Distance Run: 123.9 nm (new record!)

Saturday, May 24, 1997

In one month I'll be seeing friends and family whom I've not seen in months. There will be a lot of pomp, but I'll be content with a visit to Tim Horton's with my dad to get away from the hype. A nice bagel with strawberry cream cheese and an orange juice would not go astray right now. Yet it is senseless to think about the arrival when we still have a couple of thousand miles to go. It is the adventure of the journey, not the arrival, that matters in the end.

Today was an okay day weather-wise. It was a typical rain, drizzle and fog day in the North Atlantic. But it didn't rain enough to don foul weather gear. So we had a chance to remove the main hatch and seal up the leaks that seemed to have found their ways down onto some of our bunks. We tackled the job with silicone and neoprene, hopefully stopping our mini Niagara Falls.

The wind moved around to the southwest again during the early morning, making us brace hard to the wind. We are still holding a westerly heading, but we are affected by a lot of leeway. Steering continues to be a challenge for some and a headache to watch for me. But we plug away, slowly inching ourselves across the chart in the *nav room.

There was another sighting of whales as they crossed close to our bow—close enough for us to change our course. They quickly dove deep and we only caught a glimpse of them moving towards the horizon. The seabirds continue to follow us, feeding on our leftovers after each meal.

Tomorrow is medieval day. We'll heave to for lunch and dress up in our medieval costumes. Medieval food will be served and music played on our medieval stereo. Hopefully, no more of our state-of-the-art 21st century gear will break down on us again.

Time is passing slowly, allowing for the opportunity to think about different things. The types and varieties of ideas that one can come up with while at sea are amazing. The situation stimulates the subconscious and allows it to find expression in conscious thoughts and emotions. I have had some moving moments out here and it is funny to read back in my log and see how the experiences unfold over the weeks.

Today marks the third month that I've been on board. One more to go!

Position: 54°14.33 N; 22°20.29 W

Wind Speed: 11-14 knots

Speed: 3-4 knots

Course: 275° (WNW); 20° leeway

Sea State: moderate

Visibility: 2 miles; overcast

Sea Temp.: 13.3°C

Temp.: 10°C

Sails Set: full sail; close reaching

Distance Run: 97.0 nm

nav room: the navigation room on a ship

Sunday, May 25, 1997

Sunday, supposed to be a day of rest on board, turned out to be an overtime job for the port watch. The weather was not cooperative either, with typical North Atlantic rain, drizzle and fog. The wind was up from the southwest, stirring up large waves and a roll. The thick fog gave an eerie mood to the start of the day. My watch sat around enjoying doing nothing for most of the morning. I had a really bad headache that added to the glum atmosphere and things only got worse when we were asked to assemble the dinghy for use later in the day. I don't know who designs those things, but we were half an hour trying to figure out how to put it together. Luke, who usually does it, was sound asleep below. The frustration mounted and I found myself wishing to be anywhere but here, the first time I've felt that way since leaving Ireland.

After our watch was supposed to end, the captain decided to go over muster drills, fire drills, abandon ship drills and a real man overboard drill. It seemed to drag on for hours, though the man overboard drill went well. We sent Mark, Luke and Orlando out in the dinghy with a camera to act as a man in the water. We timed how long it would take for us to turn around and retrieve the overboard person. It also helped us to determine who should do which jobs. When we returned Nigel jumped into the water and we practiced hoisting a man out of the drink using a floating stretcher. The exercise worked well. Orlando got some great video of us sailing and of our emergency maneuvers.

After these drills we had a late medieval lunch, including a great piece of meat which was marinated in red wine and vinegar. It was an excellent meal, but we were all pretty tired and anxious to get to bed. But we were first rewarded for our efforts with a warm shower. After that it was straight to the bunks for a couple of hours of napping before we had to get up again. The wind was bitter, driving through all our clothing. I hid down in the bosun's locker, practicing some knots.

Tonight we are moving steadily towards our first way-point and the halfway marker of the voyage. David thinks we are ahead of time and going too fast. I'd rather be early than late, and anything can happen on the Grand Banks. It is not hard to sit off shore til the 24th. I say we keep dashing along. Hopefully, we will. I have galley day tomorrow—can't wait!

Position: 54°24.3 N; 24°26.1 W

Wind Speed: 180 knots SSW

Speed: 4.0 knots

Course: 285°; lots of leeway

Sea State: moderate-high waves

Visibility: poor; rain

Sea Temp.: 12.8°C

Temp.: 5°C

Sails Set: full sail; close reaching

Distance Run: 94.9 nm

Monday, May 26, 1997

It was a great galley with Nick "The Spice King" Craig. With an easy swell, things ran smoothly and with time to spare. The only hitch was that we ran out of food for ourselves at dinner. But we came through that by cooking up some pretty mean omelettes. I sit here now listening to the somber tones of the Gregorian monks as the sun is slowly setting with a shimmer of light in our path. We are barreling toward the halfway way-point, expecting to reach it tomorrow. That's where I plan to phone home and break out a flask of Newfoundland Gold and a container of Pringles. It's not a great celebration meal, but it is something that we are not used to—a treat.

Besides cooking dinner, we had a small gathering for Holy Communion. Nick, Mark, Rev. Russell and I had a small informal service around the stove. We used bread that was made on board for the first time this morning and real port. Even though it was rushed and just before dinner, it was one of the most moving spiritual experiences of my life. It was the simplicity of it. Set against a force far greater than our own, the sea, we ask to be protected like many mariners have done before us. I am sure it was a daily practice for Cabot and his crew as they crossed the Atlantic. It gives one confidence in an environment where fear of the unknown can plague you.

Position: 54°49.96 N; 26°10.6 W

Wind Speed: SSW 16.0 knots; gusty

Speed: 4.5-5.5 knots

Course: 290°

Sea State: rough

Visibility: fair-moderate

Sea Temp.: 12.8°C

Temp.: 9°C

Sails Set: full sail; close reaching

Distance Run: 75.1 nm

Tuesday, May 27, 1997

After a good night's sleep, I was ready to tackle a few jobs during the six hour watch. I ended up spending most of the day up on the main yard tallowing, oiling and preventing chafe on the mast and shrouds. In Cabot's day the ship's *rigger was in charge of all that hung above decks and would climb around the rigging without a harness. I wanted to experience the freedom of working above a rolling ship without a harness too, and it makes me feel alive.

I was also on whale watch today, pointing the direction in which they were going. We saw a few of them, and one measured almost the length of the ship. We've been lucky to see a lot of wildlife out here since we left Ireland.

The day was pretty much scot-free. We had another *Nimrod* flyby, with an airdrop to beat. It was good to get some recent magazines. On the downside, James cooked some awful chunky chicken.

Position: 59°09.1 N; 28°38.9 W
Wind Speed: W 15 knots
Speed: 3-4 knots
Course: 320°
Sea State: moderate
Visibility: very good; sunny
Sea Temp.: 10°C
Temp.: 12°C
Sails Set: full sail
Distance Run: 112.0 nm

Wednesday, May 28, 1997

IN STORM! No time to write!

Position: 55°43.03 N; 30°42.35 W
Wind Speed: SSW 40-50 knots
Speed: 2 knots
Course: 310°
Sea State: very rough; 25-foot swell
Visibility: rain; overcast
Sea Temp.: 9.3°C
Temp.: 5°C
Sails Set: forecourse
Distance Run: 10.2 nm

*rigger: a person who rigs a ship, fitting it with masts, sails and ropes

Thursday, May 29, 1997

One might consider today the aftermath, yet it is just a calm between storms. The weather that culminated yesterday began building slowly Tuesday night. By the time we got on watch at 3 a.m., the wind was 30 knots, gusting to 35 knots. We were still at full sail, the wind pushing us over hard. At 5 a.m. the hands high order was given and the other watch left their bunks to join us. The barometer had been dropping fast all night from 1015 down to 988. The wind was now gusting at 40 knots and the sea was getting much larger.

We got the lateen down first. That was easy. Then the main yard, which took the whole crew working together to take down, as the wind played havoc with the half-filled sail. Skipper diverted course downwind to neutralize the sails, but it caused the ship to roll more, throwing the main yard back and forth, the para-tackle snapping violently on the mast. When we finally got it down we quickly took off the main *drabbler and *bonnet and hoisted the yard again. We were moving along at 5 knots with the wind at our beam, but the worst was still beyond the horizon.

It was a ride til about 7 a.m.. Then the wind jumped another 10 knots and the sea rose from 10 feet to 25 to 30 feet with spray. It was hard to hold on. We were rolling 45 degrees each way, burying the *rails deep into the water. One had to be careful working down there, as it would be easy for the sea to suck you overboard.

People started to worry with this change in the weather. Blocks, lines and sails were flapping everywhere and made it hard to hear orders from across the ship. The chain of command was breaking down slowly. Crew members started giving orders themselves, a dangerous procedure. Skipper realized this and quickly took control. He told Peter to shut-up and listen to him. Everyone followed suit and we lowered the main yard, which usually takes a maximum of three minutes to do but took ten this time. The yard was flying all over, the sails lifting it into the air, and the waves dragging it under with each roll. It did not want to come down. It was almost alive with rage, like a bratty kid who really doesn't want to go to bed. We fought it to the deck, quickly furled it, and secured it so it wouldn't swing.

The waves were now breaking over the deck, Mother Nature injecting more fear into my heart every minute. I've never seen a sea like this one. It was wall to wall water. The sea was covered with white foam, the spray off the top of the waves flying horizontally through the air, stinging my face. This was a test of our teamwork, a test of the ship's ability in a storm, and a test of our threshold of fear.

By the end of the day we were left with the forecourse mainstay sail and a newly thought of lateen sail (forestay sail moved aft). The wind slowly died down, leaving us to heave around windless in a still swollen sea. These conditions make things like sleeping and eating hazardous activities. Many cups of tea have been spilled at the dinner table, and some crew members have made unexpected exits from our bunks onto the floor.

bonnet: a piece of canvas attached to a sail in light winds to increase the area of the sail

drabbler: a piece of canvas which is laced to a sail to increase its depth

rail: the upper part of a ship's bulwarks

The lull in the wind after the storm passed gave us a chance to make repairs and improvements to many parts of the ship in time for the new and deeper low expected tomorrow. We checked for chafe aloft and reinforced old and worn lines. It also gave us time to remember tactics for dealing with heavy weather, as it is confusing and dangerous to go over what to do while actually in the middle of a storm. Time is short in those situations and decisions must be made quickly.

Overall, I am happy with the way things turned out. The ship performed well and we had no major hangups in our teamwork. All this will be put to the test tomorrow when the wind will be stronger, the waves larger, and our fatigue greater.

Position: 56°00.1 N; 30°51.8 W
Wind Speed: 17 knots WNW
Speed: 2.0 knots
Course: 210°
Sea State: moderate
Visibility: good
Sea Temp.: 9.0°C
Temp.: 12°C
Sails Set: full sail, no lateen or lateen staysail
Distance Run: 43.6 nm

Hauling down a staysail halyard.

May 29, 1997. Hanging on during a gale which the captain recorded in the ship's log as "the first real blow of wind since setting out across the Atlantic," adding that "both ship and crew have passed the test well."

May 30, 1997. The ship sometimes rolled 50 or 60 degrees during this storm, so that the rails dug into the water and the deck was awash.

May 30, 1997. Fifty-foot waves such as this one photographed from the deck passed over and under us for two days.

Friday, May 30, 1997

Yesterday's storm was a walk in the park compared to the one we are in now. When our watch got on at 3 a.m., the barometer read 1017. It was at 990 by mid-afternoon. This free-fall effect was pretty cool to watch. The wind piped up a notch every time a bar was lost. The waves took a while to build, but proved to be larger than the ones experienced two days ago. The wind dropped a little in the morning, but whipped up again to a constant 40 to 45 knots. We had the foresail and lateen staysail up, keeping us from rocking too violently.

The sea was increasing by the hour, putting a lot of stress on the rigging and sails. Skipper finally decided to drop the sails, as the wind hit 60 knots. The sail drop was going to be tricky. The wind was coming from *abeam, which is a bad direction for it to be coming from for dropping that particular sail. The yard has to be detached from the mast as it gets to the mainstay so that it can move forward and lie on the *castle rails. With the wind filling the forecourse, the yard could blow away from the ship and into the drink and could actually pound a hole in the hull if caught by the waves. In order to prevent this, the skipper eased us off the wind to neutralize the sails. This way the wind wouldn't take the forecourse off the deck.

It took three people to bear the ship away and to keep it from *broaching. Just as we headed downwind, a soft wave crashed over the stern, driving water up through the rudder hole and through a window aft. We were halfway through the drop when we suddenly rounded up again, filling the sail with wind and blowing the yard away from us. It took 12 guys 15 minutes to haul the yard in and get it on the rail. The control lines on the yard and sails were useless. It took brute strength to haul the yard in and lash it down to the rail. My fingers were bleeding from holding onto the rough canvas. The wind was blowing so hard that it was almost impossible to hear the guy next to you. We were also clipped onto the ship with safety lines, which made it difficult to move around. The waves occasionally broke over us, soaking us to the bone. We were all having a great time—it was just a little scary for a few moments!

We then waited out the storm. It didn't subside til about 3 a.m. the next day. I am exhausted, but there is no rest for the weary aboard ship.

Position: 55°41.54 W; 31°54.43
Wind Speed: SSW 30-60 knots; gusty
Speed: hove to
Course: 290°
Sea State: very rough; 40 ft. swells max.
Visibility: moderate
Sea Temp.: 9.0°C
Temp.: 9.0°C
Sails Set: forecourse; struck later in the day
Distance Run: 52.8 nm

abeam: opposite the middle of the side of a ship; or, straight across a ship
broach: to turn broadside on to the sea and wind
castle: a high structure on the deck of early ships

Saturday, May 31, 1997

I will never forget today's 3 a.m. watch shift. It was still too rough to venture on deck and the *tiller was lashed. It was very dark and bitterly cold and I was fatigued from the strain and lack of sleep over the last 36 hours. I jammed my body into a corner of the ship to try to prevent myself from sliding around with the roll. Nothing on board was still and everything creaked. I barely cared about watch and wanted to sleep, but I was actually too tired to manage even that. Then I realized that it's not even June yet and my heart sank. Time stood still.

Fortunately, things started to look up as the hours wore on and the last day in May in the North Atlantic was actually a pleasant one. The swell remained, causing a few accidents and vulgarities to sound from the belly of the ship, but there wasn't a breath of wind and the temperature was a warm 13 degrees Celsius with the sun out. These conditions set in motion a large exodus of clothing that had gotten wet during the storm. The whole deck was covered in hanging clothes by lunchtime. We must have been a strange sight to the two sperm whales that passed us by in the late morning.

We had a chance to clean up the deck, check the rigging, and relax. The only excitement came when Peter lost his hat over the side and was attacked by curious seabirds until we retrieved it.

Position: 55°52.3 N; 31°37.9 W

Wind Speed: WNW 6 knots

Speed: 0.1-0.5 knots (snail slow!)

Course: 180°

Sea State: moderate-slight

Visibility: sunny (great day!)

Sea Temp.: 10.3°C

Temp.: 12°C

Sails Set: full sail; lateen staysail

Distance Run: 19.2 nm

Ireland

United Kingdom

Bristol

Newfoundland

Bonavista

Atlantic Ocean

tiller: a handle at the stern of a ship used to turn its rudder

May 31, 1997. The scene on board after a storm. We only had three or four days during the whole trip when the weather was fine enough for us to dry clothing, so we would take advantage of the opportunity when it arose and hang our damp clothes from every available line.

Anticipating a Sunday dinner of medieval cuisine with English beer on board the *Matthew*.

Sunday, June 1, 1997

We have finally made it to the month of June, with 24 days remaining til our arrival in Bonavista. The skipper welcomed June by making a deck scrub the official activity of the day. It was not a joyful occasion anymore. The fog was thick, giving us only 100 meters of visibility. It was also very cold and damp— a typical day in the North Atlantic.

We were free to relax and take a shower after the deck scrub. The shower was especially welcome because I sweated an awful lot during the many sail maneuvers that we did during the storms. We are each allotted three minutes to shower, which is tricky in a confined space with the sea still large, but nothing could prevent me from jumping in there. The shower water comes from a removable sink tap extension which dips water. We have been placing bets on who is going to be the first person to be flung from the stall, naked and wet, into the main hold. I also started a canvas bag that I'll use to keep my tools in as I collect them. My stitching is good, but needs improvement.

Today's medieval dinner was interesting. It was the first without fresh meat and vegetables, so the flavours were not exactly bursting in one's mouth. The salt meat and nut crumble that Kevin made was tasty enough when salt and a few condiments were added. After dinner we broke out some of the fresh blue cheese that was included in the last airdrop package, and ate it accompanied by a couple of bottles of port.

Rev. Russell did his Sunday sermon and Communion in fine fashion, as usual, and it was followed by a quiz contest between the two watches. The quiz was based on everything under the sun and one of the questions even asked for the middle name of the skipper's mother. Starboard watch (my team!) eventually came out on top by one question. Port watch, the sore losers, left a sloppy deck at watch change for revenge.

Position: 55°03.39 N; 33°41.27 W

Wind Speed: 19-20 knots ENE

Speed: 4-5-7 knots (depends on who's on helm)

Course: 260°

Sea State: moderate swell

Visibility: rain; overcast

Sea Temp.: 0.0°C (Labrador Current)

Temp.: 9°C

Sails Set: maincourse, forecourse, sprit

Distance Run: 85.9 nm

Monday, June 2, 1997

Misty Monday would be the best way to describe today. The Atlantic always seems to amaze me with the many different ways in which it presents itself. Today the water was emerald green, just like the sea in the Caribbean. The horizon was covered by a spooky mist. The sky was clear above us, yet we couldn't see ahead because of low lying fog. We entered the Gulf Stream, which is a whole new sailing world.

We clipped along at 4 knots—two weeks ahead of schedule. The skipper wants to slow down, which is discouraging because who wants to slow down when there are favourable winds? The last few weeks have seen the best sailing that the ship has ever experienced. Striking the sails and slowing down is very risky, but we are way ahead of schedule and arriving off the coast of Newfoundland early only to float around "Iceberg Alley" for two weeks is not what I'd call a good way to waste time. So we struck the mainsail and are now doing 3.5 knots under the foresail and spritsail.

We are currently between a high to the north and a multitude of lows which have become one large one, to the south. Both of these systems are giving us easterly winds. We expect strong winds for the next two days. We are 650 nautical miles from Bonavista, which should take about a week and a half to sail. There has been talk amongst the senior crew about what we could do to waste time if we arrive early. One idea is to visit the Hibernia offshore oil platform once it is in place on the Grand Banks. Another is to go fishing on the Banks, which Jack would love. The coast guard will be close by monitoring the ice, so we'll have that added safety and will be able to drift. Whatever we do, it will be a bit of a drag to have to sit off the coast for a week. I don't think anyone will want to do that.

Position: 54°27.2 N; 36°09.5 W

Wind Speed: ESE 19 knots

Speed: 5.0 knots

Course: 275°

Sea State: slight-moderate

Visibility: sunny-hazy

Sea Temp.: 8.3°

Temp.: 13°

Sails Set: forecourse, sprit

Distance Run: 94.0 nm

John Jack Smith, son of a schooner skipper from Grand Bank, Newfoundland, and the oldest member of the *Matthew*'s crew. Kevin O'Leary is in the background.

Tuesday, June 3, 1997

Another day with the wind at our backs, the fog covering our view of the horizon, and the sun always trying its hardest (I hope) to break through. The watches were chilly, but the longer we stood outside, the more layers of clothes we eventually pulled off. It is our second day without the mainsail and we are still making good time, although there is still a large and unpredictable swell that wreaks havoc upon the inattentive.

Everyone on board is pretty optimistic about our progress, but anything can happen. I've stopped looking at the "distance to go" section on the navigation plotter, partly because the more miles we knock off, the less sailing we will do. But I am also worried that if we do not take full advantage of these great easterly winds we could find ourselves struggling upwind, which the *Matthew* does not do well, all the way to Bonavista.

I've noticed that the focus of my thoughts during the long hours of night watch have suddenly changed from the day of arrival in Bonavista to the beauty that surrounds us and the mysteries that the ocean locks inside itself. They say that all the mysteries of the world lie deep in the belly of the blue giant, Earth's last frontier.

I spent most of the watch today working on a manrope for crew members to hold on to while climbing the ridge on the exterior of the bow to access the anchor chain. The plans were drawn up with Terry's help and included a main line and three anchoring lines. It worked out pretty well and I'm happy with the way it looks.

We had homemade pizza instead of chunky chicken today. The duo of Nigel and Steve made it from scratch, much to the pleasure of our taste buds. We were all stuffed, which is an odd thing on a Tuesday night, and sat to reflect afterwards. It was a great way to end a productive day and precede a short but much needed sleep.

Position: 54°08.47 N; 38°48.41 W

Wind Speed: 19-24 knots; force 5-6

Speed: 4-5 knots

Course: 275°

Sea State: moderate

Visibility: fair-poor; heavy fog-hazy

Sea Temp.: 8.3°C

Temp.: 9-10°C

Sails Set: forecourse, spritsail

Distance Run: 102.8 nm

Wednesday, June 4, 1997

A big day in the galley has come to a close with the serving of Orlando's birthday cake and shots of tequila to wash it down. With galley duty over with, I had a chance to make my first call home. I chose the 4th because it is halfway in time from the departure in Ireland to the arrival in Bonavista. It was a little goal I set for myself by breaking the trip down into sections. This was prompted by the many emotions that accumulated during the final few hours before departure, so that I felt like I needed something specific to work towards. It seems to have worked well because most of the fears that I harboured have slowly turned to vapor and have been released and the feeling of accomplishment at having reached this first goal is intoxicating. I downed some rum and had a few Pringles chips to celebrate its achievement—not much of a celebration, but something meaningful nonetheless.

We had our fist visit by Canadians today. An Aurora surveillance aircraft out on patrol buzzed us a few times to welcome us to Canadian waters—well, almost. It was good to hear a new Canadian voice over the radio.

Well, there are only about 20 days left, with two more turns on galley and a bit of rigging still to be done.

Position: 53°33.8 N; 42°07.3 W

Wind Speed: E 19-20 knots

Speed: 3.1 knots

Course: 260°

Sea State: moderate swell (hell in the galley)

Visibility: moderate; foggy horizon

Sea Temp.: 8.0°C

Temp.: 10°C

Sails Set: forecourse, sprit

Distance Run: 77.4 nm

Newfoundland

Bonavista

Ireland

United Kingdom

Bristol

Atlantic Ocean

Thursday, June 5, 1997

Another usual day on board with the usual occurrences. Getting up for the 3 a.m. watch after a day of galley was tough. I didn't get a lot of sleep and moved slowly onto deck. The wind was frosty, cutting right through the layers of my clothing to chill my bones. We had our usual deck scrub at 6 a.m. and finished the watch off with a lackluster breakfast courtesy of James and Mark. The watches are getting harder and harder to do as time wears on. We have been at this for four and a half weeks straight, 24 hours a day, seven days a week with hardly any breaks.

I plan to catch up on lost sleep when I get home, but somehow I think that the habit of getting up for watch at weird hours of the day will carry over to life on land, causing havoc even when I finally leave the ship. At least I won't be eating the dehydrated and pre-prepared food again. That is one aspect of this trip that I absolutely will not miss. We have almost run out of fresh food; "bomb-proof," "rot-proof" cabbage, lemons, apples and oranges are all that remain. We have been eating more and more tin stuff, and it's not that bad. Considering what was available in terms of long lasting food in the 1400's, we all eat like kings.

Our starboard deck scrub team finished the last section of dirty deck during day watch. The wood looks great and we celebrated by drinking a bottle of champagne which Peter had stowed away. We were then visited by a pod of about 50 pilot whales. The marine life has increased as we get closer to shore and we are keeping track of the variety of wildlife species in a special log.

We decided today that we will tack on 200 miles and go visit the Hibernia oil platform which is about 200-300 miles south of us. At the present speed we'll all be old and gray by the time we meet it, but hopefully the wind will freshen and increase our speed from a snail's pace.

Position: 52°49.6 N; 42°40 W

Wind Speed: N-NE 10-14 knots; force 4

Speed: 2.5-3.5 knots

Course: 250°

Sea State: slight with moderate cross swell

Visibility: fair-good; can see the horizon

Sails Set: forecourse, spritsail

Distance Run: 69.8 nm

Friday, June 6, 1997

I think that every day is the same out here on the Grand Banks. The weather was cool, gray and windless again. The lone seal that watched us all day probably wondered why we are all the way out here, and we wondered the same thing about him. That pod of pilot whales roamed by us again today on a fast track to nowhere, from my point of view. We sat like a cork all day, bobbing in the swell from a low far, far away. With the two staysails up for stability, we zoomed at 0.5 knots in every direction.

Deck work was slow, but I finished some tasks and started to make mats to prevent the foresail tack blocks from scraping off the deck. It took me about 40 minutes to get the first pattern right and then double it up. I didn't get it finished til the end of the watch, but it was worth the wait. They look good and work well. The canvas work is also coming along great. Matt and Russell are working like they are in a sweat shop to produce items like bags, covers and holders.

The excitement at lunch today was the discovery of a couple of cans of Pringles chips. They didn't last long, as they are a rare and valuable food out here that should not be wasted. Once you pop, you can't stop!

I've been gradually feeling more tired after all of these weeks. I'm looking forward to my next galley day when I get to sleep in. I wish I was in the land of nod now!

Position: 52°13.6 N; 43°07.1 W

Wind Speed: NW 6.0 knots

Speed: 0.0 knots

Course: self-steering

Sea State: calm swell

Visibility: good

Temp.: 10°C

Sails Set: none

Distance Run: 33.2 nm

James Roy and I tackle one of the ceaseless rigging jobs.

Saturday, June 7, 1997

The ocean at night. Alive. Bright. Unpredictable. Breathtaking. Unforgettable. All of these come to mind during this night watch. With a flat sea, calm wind, and a pleasant roll, the *Matthew* slowly slips through the icy water, leaving its signature in the fluorescent flashes of green neon light exploding all around the ship. Misty rain falls on the water, setting off a billion-watt light show—a comet in the sea. Cabot's men must have been taken aback by the same show of natural beauty as they crossed the Atlantic. That is a common element of these two voyages: the sailing is still the same and the environment both spectacular and unforgiving, just as it was 500 years ago. Time is at a standstill out here. It could be the year 1059. We have only the planes that race each other high in the night sky to remind us of our place in time. Some of us do not look up, preferring instead to imagine.

The ocean leaves a mark on everyone's soul. It is during these moments at night when the number of days left to port do not matter. If every night was like this one nobody would live on land. I am fortunate to be one of only a few people to see the sea in this surreal state. One can only become connected with the sea, breathing in the salt and letting it flow through the veins.

Position: 51°47.58 N; 43°00.59 W

Wind Speed: E 14.0 knots

Speed: 1.0 knots

Course: 250°

Sea State: slight

Visibility: low cloud

Temp.: 12°C

Sails Set: main, forecourse, sprit

Distance Run: 16.4 nm

Paul Venton and Mark Chislet clad in the usual daily attire of the *Matthew* crew. Even when we wore six or seven layers of clothing the cold and wet conditions chilled us.

June 8, 1997. My first bath in five weeks—a dip into the Atlantic with a life ring— left me numb with cold but refreshed.

Sunday, June 8, 1997

The wind shifted around to the northwest today and piped up to about 20 knots, blowing bitterly through our windproof clothing. We set all sails, which had been neatly folded hours before. It was good, though, to feel the ship heel over again and groan as the air passed through the rigging.

Earlier in the day the water was flat and the air was warm—just right for the inaugural "*Matthew* Voyage Polar Dip." With some hesitation, Paul, Pete and I finally dove off the *forecastle, plunging deep into the dark, murky Atlantic. The shock was incredible, breathtaking, and my heart was in my throat. I was both excited and scared. The sound of feeding whales came from only half a kilometer away, and I quickly made for the ship, full stroke. The water was freezing (10°C), but surprisingly refreshing. It was the first time in five weeks that I had the chance to be fully immersed in water. I could feel the salt lifting the dirt from my skin.

The guys on board were laughing away at my inability to coordinate speech. After a couple more dives it was picture time. Skipper gave me his camera and I jumped in the water and took a few snaps. In total, we spent about five minutes in the water—the time it takes for someone to enter deep hypothermia in these waters. Although I could not feel any layer of my skin, I was refreshed and ready for a warm three minute shower to get the blood flowing again. It was a good way to end a watch during which we had hauled up all the floorboards from down below, cleaned them along with the bilges and the deck, and returned them to their places. It was Hell Sunday, but everything got cleaned and now smells good.

Position: 51°14.8 N; 43°54.8 W

Wind Speed: NNW 4 knots

Speed: 0.0 knots

Course: 245°

Sea State: calm

Visibility: cloudy-overcast

Sails Set: none

Distance Run: 38.4 nm

forecastle: the upper deck in front of the foremast of a ship

Monday, June 9, 1997

This has been an unremarkable day which began with a deck scrub. The winds were fresh from the north and sperm whales played in our wake. The time is moving a lot slower now, causing some to get "Channel fever."

There is a stomach bug on board and Jerry is its latest victim. With all of us living in such close proximity, this ship is an ideal place for a virus to circulate. It seems to drain its victims' energy, so stricken crew members are granted a night without having to go on watch. Of course, the medical team on board, consisting of two doctors and a paramedic, is well prepared to handle any health problems.

Anything can happen and it is important that we are prepared to deal with a wide range of situations. The only real accident since we left Bristol occurred when the captain caught his thumb in his cabin doorframe after the door unlatched when the shipped rolled violently. His thumb was painfully split and required stitches. This injury prevented him from participating in the sail maneuvers he loves. I pray that we will all remain safe for the rest of the trip.

Position: 50°36.17 N; 43°44.60 W

Wind Speed: W 13.0 knots

Speed: 2.0 knots

Course: 220°

Distance Run: 44.7 nm

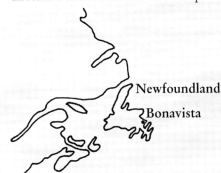

Newfoundland

Bonavista

Atlantic Ocean

Ireland

United Kingdom

Bristol

Tuesday, June 10, 1997

With the sun high in the sky, I broke out my trusty sextant to get a lesson from Jack, who is virtually a human GPS (global positioning system) after 60 years' experience at navigating by the sun and stars. He can pinpoint our position on this vast ocean in just a few minutes. It was high time for me to take advantage of his wealth of knowledge and "shoot the sun." Trying to get an accurate fix on the sun is challenging on a stable boat—and next to impossible on the *Matthew*. I spent most of my time chasing the sun instead of shooting it!

I contemplated the diversity of our crew's knowledge and experience while trying to digest my favourite meal of chunky chicken this evening. When we first set out on this trip I was worried that some crew members' inexperience at sea might be dangerous in the long run, but now I realize that we each excel at certain skills and we have been learning from each other. I have learned about the production of a television show, efficient woodworking and cooking—and admittedly still have lots to learn on the latter.

Position: 50°40.2 N; 44°04.0 W
Distance Run: 54.3 nm

John Jack Smith and I shooting the sun off the coast of Ireland.

Wednesday, June 11, 1997

The last few days have seen many a sail change, and today was no different. We have taken the bonnets off so many times that most of the crew could do it in their sleep. Sometimes I think we do! The wind has slowly backed around to the south, which allows us to steer an east-northeast course.

The pace is slow but steady, much as it would have been in Cabot's day. Like us, Cabot would have definitely noticed the difference when he entered the green waters of the Gulf Stream. However, he would not have seen the amount of garbage it now carries from North America. The crew has spotted everything from plastic bags to a soccer ball. It is sad to see how this ocean environment has been tarnished. I guess that people figure that the ocean will pull the garbage into its depths to rot, but this is not necessarily the case. Some days it is as if we are passing through a dump.

Position: 51°25.0 N; 44°49.9 W

Distance Run: 46.9 nm

Sailing full and by.

Thursday, June 12, 1997

Yet another wet day as a front moves overhead, robbing us of wind and our good spirits and leaving us adrift in a complex system of lows. It is hard to motivate myself to face days like this. Rising from a warm sleeping bag only to pull on damp and smelly clothing is even more difficult than eating chunky chicken cooked by James and Mark.

I think that putting on seven layers of clothing while remaining balanced on a rolling ship should become an official Olympic sport, with extra marks awarded to competitors who can put on pants without falling and swearing. On board the *Matthew* this routine begins with a member of the "awake" watch flicking on all the lights (a cruel form of torture), and preceding to each bunk to inform its occupant "It's that time!" in a mockingly cheerful voice. The first task for a rising crew member is to free himself from whatever materials he had packed around his body before going to sleep to avoid being rolled onto the floor. Then the transition from the warm bunk to the cool ocean air begins. Deciding what to wear is never a problem, although trying to remember where you put it three hours ago often is. Our clothes seem to go on little adventures of their own while we sleep, and tend to end up under a leak.

My bunk is in the corner by the engine, along with Mark's, Peter's and Steve's. We emerge from our sleeping bags at intervals, making it easier to coexist in the little room we have. Mark always gets up first and heads directly for his caffeine and chocolate fix. And I am always last. I wait until there are just five minutes to watch change and then race to get my clothes on and turn up on deck half dressed and half awake. But the cold air brings me around in a hurry, and makes me look forward to being the one to issue the wake-up calls three hours later.

Position: 51°32.8 N; 45°54.8 W

Distance Run: 56.4 nm

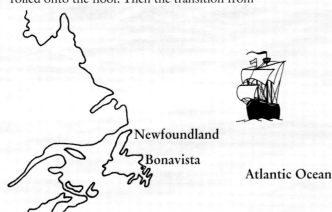

Newfoundland

Bonavista

Atlantic Ocean

Ireland

United Kingdom

Bristol

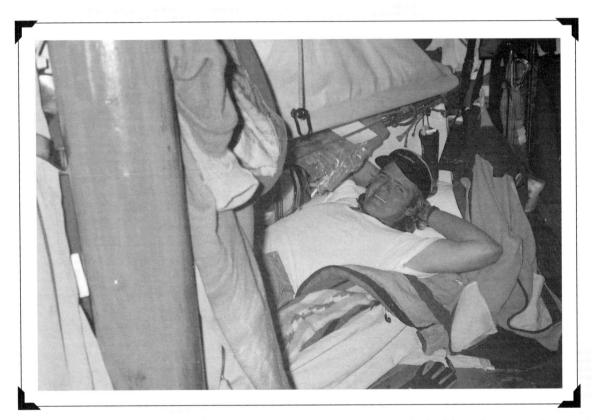

My bunk was the only space on the ship that I could call my own. The buildup of seven weeks' worth of clothes and gear kept me from rolling out of bed.

Friday, June 13, 1997

The day started off beautifully with a hazy sunrise and weird weather. It all moved off eventually, leaving a clear blue sky and warm temperature—an odd day here on the Banks. Unfortunately, I had to spend it below, cooking in the hot galley. It is Friday the 13th and Nick and I expected the worst. The weather was fine, so there was no violent rolling. Everything was going great until the afternoon, when I finished scrubbing and peeling about forty potatoes. When I tried to pour the dirty water out of the pot that they were in, I tipped it too much and about 25 potatoes hit the water and sunk within seconds. Nick screamed and the rest of the crew laughed their heads off. I cried and started all over again.

It was also another perfect day for a coastguard flyover. Steve and Orlando did their thing, beaming up images shot over the last week. After that the twin engine plane did a couple of low level passes, getting closer and closer each time. It was good to hear a Canadian voice on the radio again.

Supper turned out great. We made a beef stew that won the hearts of all. It was followed by a double fudge cake that had them calling for seconds. We ended our day by breaking out a secret stash of Pringles, Newfoundland Gold Rum, and orange juice. It was eaten on deck in the glow of a beautiful sunset.

A group of intermittent clouds is signaling bad weather ahead. 200 miles to go and we are now officially in CANADA! And I'm in need of a full night's sleep.

Position: 50°42.3 N; 47°4.8 W
Distance Run: 60.8 nm

Nick Craig and I enjoy a glass of Newfoundland Gold Rum after a long day in the galley.

Saturday, June 14, 1997

The full night's sleep that I had hoped for did not materialize. Instead, I woke up every time there was a little roll, a watch change, or a chill that found its way into my sleeping bag. It was very frustrating because I am still really tired from not having a real break in over a month. After reluctantly rolling out of bed at 6:30 a.m., I had an interesting breakfast of bread and raisins. I was not going to attempt to eat James's oatmeal.

The weather was wet and windy, leaving us to take care of most tasks below decks. I worked on the canvas cover for this log for most of the day. The others mostly worked on the canvas flag holder that will live in the nav room after it is completed. Russell Owen is working at his top speed to get it done. We also spent a lot of time doing sail maneuvers. We found a new way to take the bonnet and drabbler off the mainsail without dropping the main yard to the deck. It is faster, easier and more efficient.

I am very tired now. The willpower to even get out of bed is harder to muster. The stomach bug is going around and I'm worried that I may get it. We are moving along steadily, but it seems like we are going nowhere. The miles and the days are getting longer. We've been at sea for a long time and are missing home quite a lot now.

Position: 50°19.2 N; 48°01.6 W
Wind Speed: SSW 15 knots
Speed: 1.5 knots
Course: 300°
Sea State: slight swell
Visibility: poor; fog
Sea Temp.: 7.8°C
Temp.: 5.0°C
Sails Set: main, forecourse, sprit
Distance Run: 54.3 nm

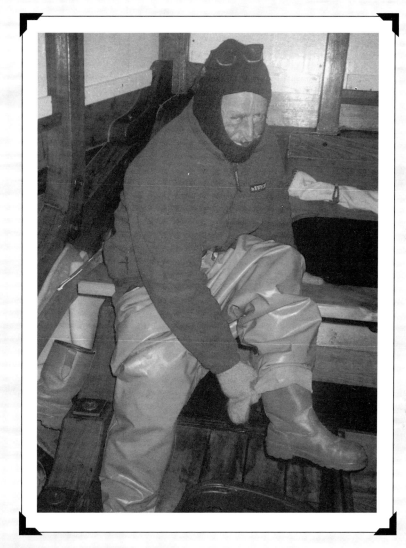

Rev. Russell Owen during a night watch. Russell seemed to
have a difficult time putting on and removing foul weather gear.
Once we found him rolling around on the deck trying to pull
on his boots.

Sunday, June 15, 1997

This morning's watch at 3 a.m. was greeted by near freezing temperatures, howling winds, dense fog and a confused sea. Add the rain squalls that move through in rapid succession, and you have a poor way to start the day. Half of our watch shift was spent on sail maneuvers, the other on iceberg watch and the fun job of scrubbing the deck. I won't miss that. I had to go gloveless because my gloves were wet. By the end of watch my hands were a light shade of blue and cramped tight with cold. It took some minutes over the stove to move them again. That's okay because I love doing that kind of thing—getting out there and experiencing things to the max.

Today Paul and Martin were on galley duty. The food was excellent, even though it was a medieval recipe from a can. The trivia game was won by the port watch in a tiebreaker. It was their first win and they gloried in it.

Position: 50°32.03 N; 49°30.20 W

Wind Speed: SW 23 knots

Speed: 2.0 knots

Course: 270°

Sea State: moderate

Sails Set: mainstay, *mizzen staysail

Distance Run: 57.5 nm

Newfoundland

Bonavista

Atlantic Ocean

Ireland

United Kingdom

Bristol

mizzen: mizzenmast; the mast closest to the stern of a two- or three-masted sailing vessel; or, the fore-and-aft sail on the mizzenmast

Monday, June 16, 1997

Blue sky? That was the question we were asking ourselves as the rumor spread amongst the crew. After getting ready for watch, we stumbled up on deck to be greeted by a blue day and a bitter northerly wind. There was a catch, I guess, as the temperature didn't get above 6 degrees Celsius. The sunshine allowed us to bring all the damp gear collected over the last few foggy days to the deck to dry. My sleeping bag was a wreck and benefitted from an airing out.

The nice weather allowed us to touch up the yards with tar and oil, do some painting work, ladder sanding and oiling, and some mast oiling. After a certain amount of time the yard rubbing on the mast causes a massive degree of chafe, almost eating through the wood. We sand down the chafed areas and oil them thoroughly to keep the water from causing the wood to rot. With only a small swell, Gerry had the pleasure of going up to the top of the mizzen mast and repairing the damage up there. At more than 200 pounds, he wasn't the best candidate to go up, but after four of us heaved and hauled for a few minutes he was perched at the top, humming away.

It was also the start of the week and the final galley days. Jack and Matthew are the first galley crew to escape from the clutches of that shipboard duty. Unfortunately, Sunday is my last galley day, the hell day in the galley world. I hope this weather keeps up.

Position: 50°24.2 N; 49°52.2 W

Wind Speed: SW 12 knots

Course: 220°

Sea State: slight swell

Visibility: good; sunny

Sails Set: main; mizzen staysail; motor

Distance Run: 33.1 nm

palm: a leather pad with a metal plate in the center worn over the palm of the hand and used much like a thimble when sewing sails or related items

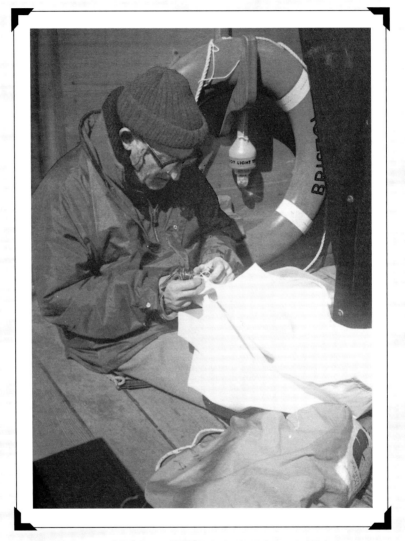

Many of us had primary jobs on board. Rev. Russell Owen was a sailmaker and worked on the same flag holder for the entire journey, but never finished it. Now he doesn't want to see another *palm and needle ever again!

Tuesday, June 17, 1997

Another bright, sunny day with a beautiful sunrise. The wind is still bitterly cold and has increased from the southwest to about 25 knots. It was a great day for photos, and as the coastguard plane flew in for the BBC's final uplink, we broke out our cameras. We set a few ceremonial flags and our sails bounced with the gust as the bow punched into the waves. It was a quiet celebration of just one week remaining in the voyage. With just days of our trip left, a bit of "Channel fever" has come over the crew, and everyone is talking about family, the arrival and what they miss most about home.

Night watches are quietly passed thinking about what one might be doing in a week's time. The guys on Cabot's crew didn't have that luxury—or curse, depending on how you look at it. They didn't know when they were going to arrive, so it must have been extra joyful for them. We are also sailing into the unknown, as we have no idea of what to expect when we get to Bonavista. David says it's going to be big, but the only big things we are used to are waves and whales.

With a less than favourable forecast ahead, we are tracking north of west, towards St. Anthony. This may be like the first week of the voyage, tirelessly spent going nowhere. It will be a real test of the crew and the ship to survive this already emotionally exhausting week.

Position: 50° 19.9 N; 50° 49.05 W
Wind Speed: SW 21 knots
Speed: 2.0 knots
Course: 290°
Sea State: choppy swell
Visibility: good
Sails Set: full sail
Distance Run: 63 nm

Wednesday, June 18, 1997

Hello fog, rain and drizzle. Goodbye sun, sky and horizon. The first part of the morning was spent milling around trying to digest Kevin's pancake breakfast. The rain eventually subsided, as did the wind, prompting us to put on the forecourse bonnet. The air was saturated with the smell of fish. There wasn't much deck work and a lot of the day was wasted on sail maneuvers. We decided to change course from northwest to southeast. The ship is having a hard time punching through the waves as there is a lack of wind to drive her. These kinds of watches make the time creep by more slowly.

We are just 120 miles from Bonavista, but going at only a snail's pace. By the time we got on night watch at 19:00 hours, the wind had completely faded and we were under steam on a tired course to Bonavista at about 2 knots. It was a surreal evening with deathly fog cloaking our sails and whispers behind the odd wisp of wind. It left me a little messed up chronologically— Am I here or there in time? I guess it does not really matter.

David talked to us about some of the events that are planned for our arrival in Bonavista. It is all that is on everyone's mind. I fear people's last days will be wasted on thinking about the future and not appreciating the beauty of the present. Here we are sailing in water drenched in maritime history, in weather quite like no other place, and in an area known to leave a mark on the men who dare to tackle it. It is only natural, I guess, to dream of seeing and doing things that we haven't been able to do for a long time. I was even caught dreaming after listening to Nightline on VOCM on the battery-operated radio. People were phoning in and expressing their delight, excitement, regrets, complaints and concerns about the whole Cabot celebration. It was the first time that I got the gist of what people really feel about the whole project at home in Newfoundland. It was a little weird.

I can't sleep.

Position: 50°30.8 N; 50°49.3 W

Wind Speed: WSW 16 knots

Course: 170°

Sea State: moderate

Visibility: poor; fog

Sails Set: main; mizzen staysail

Distance Run: 62.3 nm

Bonavista

Newfoundland

Atlantic Ocean

Thursday, June 19, 1997

Nick was the first to arrive into the unwelcoming weather for watch this evening. The fog is so thick that we can see it crawling over the deck, soaking everything in its path. The condensation runs down the face of the lonely soul who is helming the ship. The smell of wet cotton, socks, men and five weeks' supply of dehydrated food hangs in the air of the main hold. The smell is as thick as the fog on the deck.

With less than a week to go, people are testy and easily ticked off. The weather has prevented the completion of a lot of work above decks. The other riggers and I are jobless, left to fiddle with line and canvas. The feeling among the watch captains is that we should only spend watch time on ship's work. If my work is prevented, then what am I to do? It has ruined morale, as they find unpleasant jobs for us to do. The captain caught some guys working away on personal bags at 3 a.m. and made them take all the cushion covers out of the galley and handwash them in the miserable morning weather. That's not a great way to stir morale after seven weeks at sea.

The night is bright, as the fog acts like a nightlight, absorbing all available light. The waves are steep, causing the ship to roll violently from side to side. Without the mainsail up, stability is lost. Jack comments that this is the worst night for ship performance of the whole voyage. With about 100 miles to go, we are exactly where we were last night after turning off the engine in a dead lull—a questionable maneuver. I have been suffering from sleeplessness and am often driven to drink—literally. A little rum can put anyone out.

The weather is draining us all. Hold on boys, hold on.

Position: 50°14.7 N; 51°33.2 W

Wind Speed: 20-25 knots SW/SSW

Speed: 2.5-3.5 knots

Course: 280°

Sea State: 1-2 m; light swell

Visibility: 50-100 yards; poor; thick fog

Sea Temp.: 4.7°C

Temp.: 5-7°C

Sails Set: lateen, mainsail, forecourse

Distance Run: 28.3 nm

June 20, 1997. The first iceberg sighted on the voyage. When it appeared on our radar screen we thought it was another ship, but the fog lifted suddenly and Mark Chislet spotted this monster a mile off our starboard beam. It split in half just as we were leaving.

Friday, June 20, 1997

With the new day came a new attitude for the North Atlantic. As the fog that has drenched the ship for the last couple of days cleared, blue horizons appeared in each direction. We were monitoring a huge contact on the radar screen which we believed to be a coastguard ship keeping a quiet eye on us. As the fog rolled back Mark spotted a huge iceberg off the starboard beam. We couldn't believe the size of it. For most of the crew it was their first berg. The ocean seemed to be saying, "Don't mess with me!" in a subtle kind of way. We had easily assumed that the berg was a ship and had paid it no mind. The *growlers that periodically showed themselves, as if they were playing hid and seek, covered the perimeter.

The iceberg was a safe distance of about two and a half miles away. But because this is a "showboat," David decided to lose the miles we've been trying to gain in the last couple of days and motor closer to the thing for a photo shoot. Mark, Orlando and Luke got some footage of the ship sailing by the berg. It was a lovely, clear day, and the green essence of the iceberg shimmered in the sun. It was a beautiful sight. The side fell off the berg as we were leaving, causing a huge surge of water and growlers to spread around the remains.

The rest of the day was extraordinary. The sunset was the best of the trip, with a clear west horizon. A weather system to the east was covered by a variety of different clouds, which changed colour as the sun set. It is a moonlit night for us as we keep watch at the bow for growlers.

Position: 50°27.6 N; 52°39.9 W

Wind Speed: 15 knots WSW

Speed: 2.5 knots

Course: 280°

Sea State: moderate; choppy

Visibility: clearing fog; bright, sunny day

Sails Set: forecourse, main, lateen, sprit

Distance Run: 55.7 nm

Bonavista

Newfoundland

Atlantic Ocean

Ireland

United Kingdom

Bristol

growlers: pieces of floating ice which have broken off an iceberg

June 20, 1997. Changing a sail off the coast of Newfoundland with the best sunset of the voyage in the background.

The Englishmen of the crew loved tea and every hour someone would go down to the galley to put a pot to boil and then serve it. There were a few times when the roll of the ship sent the tea carrier and his load sprawling across the deck. Here Paul Venton delivers a cup safely to me.

June 21, 1997. The Canadian Coastguard ship *Leonard J. Cowley* welcomed us into Canadian waters. I was on galley duty on the *Matthew* that day and remember the smells of fresh food being cooked which drifted from the coastguard ship and made me envious of its crew.

Saturday, June 21, 1997

It is hard to believe that we are only three days from Bonavista, but the excitement on shore and sea is building. The coastguard ship *Leonard J. Cowley* was the first to officially welcome us to Canadian waters. It appeared during my morning sunrise watch, hovering on the horizon like an iceberg. But eventually the red hull came into view, much to the surprise of Russell, who was on iceberg watch and shouted "Iceberg!" ten minutes after we had determined that it was a ship. It was pretty funny. It hovered around us for a while and then left as quietly as it had come.

We hoisted full sail and made a southerly course towards Bonavista until the wind died, leaving us about 50 miles away. They didn't believe me when I said that we have nice weather in Newfoundland, but the sun shone down on us all day, the longest of the year. This allowed us to take up the *fo'c'sle boards and clean the bilge. Lots of fun! After cleaning out tons of dirt that had found its way down there over the last couple of weeks, we sanded and varnished the boards and replaced them.

Mark had his radio tuned to VOCM all the while we were working. The English find the type of radio over here amusing. They couldn't believe that there were live reports from a paint shop in Bonavista. The airways are buzzing with information about the *Matthew* arrival and that is almost our only indication of the amount of interest in the province. When I phoned home tonight my parents said that things were looking very impressive. A lot of people will be watching us. It will be a little weird to be on the television and too much attention can go to one's head.

The tension between the crew and senior crew continues to boil. I think some of the guys on my watch have totally exasperated Terry, our watch captain. He has turned into a stone cold navy man. He doesn't even smile any more. Maybe he has Channel fever.

I am okay, but the prospect of galley duty tomorrow doesn't amuse me. Hopefully all will go well, as it will be a full ship cleaning day.

Position: 50°27.6 N; 52°39.9 W

Wind Speed: W 16 knots

Course: 190°

Sea State: moderate; slow moving

Visibility: good; weather change (fog out, fun in!)

Sails Set: full sail

Distance Run: 55.7 nm

fo'c'sle: forecastle; the upper deck in front of the foremast of a ship

Sunday, June 22, 1997

Since it is "Super Sunday," we performed a full ship cleaning as usual, but this time the results had to be fit for a queen, literally! All the floor boards were removed from below and brought up onto the deck to be scrubbed. The bilge was still soaked with hydraulic oil which spilled in there after one of the lines leading to the propellers burst under Kevin's bunk. Rev. Russell feel asleep while he was cleaning in there, but was suddenly awakened when he dropped a scrub brush on his own foot.

Nick and I completed our final stint in the galley of the trip, using the last can of meat on board for this evening's medieval dinner. I am writing this log entry now in the midst of a crew party, surrounded by members of the elite "Medieval Atlantic Crossing Club" who are crucifying Frank Sinatra's "New York, New York." I don't see a Grammy nomination in their futures! We are hove to, relaxing for the first time since the beginning of the voyage, and are drinking the rest of the brandy in the keg. With everyone enjoying this less than routine celebration, night watch will be conducted by whomever is still up. I think I'll sleep well tonight.

Position: 49°33.5 N; 52°32.4 W

Wind Speed: WNW 6 knots

Speed: 0-5 knots

Course: 210°

Sea State: slight

Visibility: good; sunny

Sails Set: full sail

Distance Run: 49.6 nm

I served my last galley duty on this day and surprised the crew by serving my Aunt Effie's homemade cookies, which I warmed in the oven. They were quite a treat and everyone loved them.

Monday, June 23, 1997

Other people, other faces! As the crew slowly arose after last night's party the word spread that we were going to have visitors later in the day. Some pretty pathetic souls stumbled onto the deck, some running for the rails and others waiting in the small line that had formed around the rudder hole, the designated bladder relief area. As I was on galley duty last night my morning wasn't as rough as some of the other guys', and Kevin and I were assigned to tar the last two blocks on the ship, which were, of course, also the hardest to reach. We spent half an hour swinging around, spilling tar and emitting an odd vulgarity before we were told that the Royal Canadian Mounted Police were on their way to the ship to search for bombs.

Before long three divers, three police officers and a German Shepherd came from alongside the Canadian Coastguard ship *Leonard J. Cowley*. Usually one would be a little anxious about having a police search team arrive, but they were a welcome sight as they were the first faces apart from those of the crew that we have seen in six weeks. The whole time that they were on board we just kept staring at them and Dillon, the RCMP dog, who actually had an adventure just trying to get on board the *Matthew*. He was lowered over the side of the coastguard ship and driven at high speed to our vessel. Getting a frightened German Shepherd out of a dinghy over the high rails of the *Matthew* is no easy task. It was a sight to see, with four huge RCMP officers equipped with guns and bomb gear trying to hoist the dog over the side with no cooperation from either the creature or the swell that was pushing the two vessels away from each other.

We talked the officers' ears off for an hour longer than they were supposed to be on board. It was good to hear Canadian voices again and they told us of the excitement in Bonavista. We are still oblivious to that. Then they threw Dillon back in the boat and headed to the *Cowley*, leaving behind 19 smelly, tired and hung-over sailors who will complete this transatlantic trip tomorrow. I am sure that these last 24 hours will prove to be the longest of the voyage.

Position: 49° 22.1 N; 53° 04 W

Wind Speed: 2-5 knots SE

Speed: 0.5 knots

Course: 220°

Distance Run: 28.4 nm

Dillon the dog and the rest of the RCMP search team were actually a welcome sight.

June 24, 1997. I was on cannon duty for the arrival in Bonavista. Just after this photo was taken we passed through the narrows and in front of the *Northern Ranger*. There were people waving on the bow and I accidentally set the cannon off in their direction in all the excitement. I had the cannon lighter taken away from me after that!

Tuesday, June 24, 1997

I will start with the words that I used to conclude yesterday's log entry: this has been the longest 24 hours of the voyage. The wind piped up to a gale as we approached Bonavista. When I came on watch at 11 p.m. we could see the lights of the harbour. A feeling of accomplishment mixed with sadness swept through me, but it quickly disappeared when I learned that we were drifting towards the rocks! Sails were set and trimmed as we chose a course away from Bonavista. The wind was bitterly cold, finding its way through every layer of my "wind-proof" clothing. Yet my soul was warm and everyone was in an upbeat mood in anticipation of the arrival.

My watch recalled special memories of the trip as we all sat around the upper deck. About halfway through the watch Rev. Russell finally got all his gear on and made it up on deck in time to tell one of the many stories from his repertoire. Someone brought up some popcorn, but if you tried to grab a handful you ended up with only a couple of kernels as the wind whisked it away.

Dawn approached and Rev. Russell began counting the minutes instead of the days. He was happy to be finally sailing into port after 52 days at sea. During the voyage he kept us all focused and safe by praying for us every day.

Much to the delight of the crew, we didn't start the last day of the trip with a traditional deck scrub. The captain had special deck cleaning solutions delivered to the ship, and we were equipped with gloves and gas masks to dilute a layer of wood on the deck and return it to its original luster.

We were called below for a final meeting at 11:40 a.m. to discuss procedure and our jobs for the arrival, concluding with a prayer. With that, we turned the ship around and headed towards Bonavista at 9 knots, dodging bits of icebergs all the way. Much of the coastline was covered in fog, and I had worried the whole morning that the weather would keep people away from the arrival festivities, but two miles from the harbour the rugged shoreline broke into our view, dotted with red, yellow, blue and green raincoats. I knew that my mother was there somewhere because I could hear her voice. Everyone on board was taken aback and our adrenaline levels soared with the excitement.

After following the shoreline, the question of where the entrance to the harbour was arose, as it was not visible from sea. We already had to concern ourselves with the icebergs and the wind that was pushing us on, so we welcomed the coastguard rescue boats which joined us for safety, although the accompanying helicopter had bad timing and drowned out orders during sail maneuvers. But we had done these together a hundred times and everyone knew his own job as well as that of the guy next to him. The sail drop was smooth and quick and we soon found ourselves at the mouth of the harbour.

The cannons were loaded, positions manned and, at the cue of the musicians the Irish Descendants, we made our entrance. As we sailed into the harbour I remembered something that I once read: "The past is not dead history; it is the living material out of which man makes the present and builds the future." That applies

June 24, 1997. My mom was somewhere in the mass of people who had come to greet the *Matthew* at Bonavista and I could hear her from about a mile offshore. Here we were waiting for Queen Elizabeth to arrive for the celebration.

to this *Matthew* voyage. John Cabot and his crew made an incredible transatlantic voyage 500 years ago and we have recreated the adventure. And my home province, Newfoundland, has such an incredibly rich history which is kept alive through this anniversary celebration, which will in turn create opportunities for the future of the province.

The mouth of the harbour was very small and as we passed through it felt as if we could reach out and touch the people on the breakwater. There were so many familiar faces and our emotions raced. Our families stood at dockside holding signs, waving and crying. Among them were particular relatives whose presence was a surprise for some of the crew. Before we left Bristol the *Matthew* Project administrators had said that the English crew members' return trips would be paid for, but now they surprised them by bringing their girlfriends, wives and kids to Newfoundland.

After we had passed through the breakwater things came to a halt when we learned that Queen Elizabeth had not yet arrived. But in all the excitement I accidentally fired my cannon in the face of a guy who was standing on the bow of the *Northern Ranger*. He got quite a surprise when a cloud of smoke exploded in front of him and I got into a little bit of trouble for that move!

We were given the green light to tie up and jumped ashore into awaiting arms. My family was there, including my two grandfathers. After all the hugs I broke out a small bottle of scotch and a Tim Horton's donut to celebrate the arrival.

Our entrance to Bonavista has been captured on tape for all to see, and my description is no better. What is contained in the pages of this log will probably be old news in a few years. But it is an honest account of what the camera didn't show. I have had the time of my life, and I have become a better person. Hopefully the *Matthew* will cast its magic spell on everyone who greets it.

Position: Bonavista, Newfoundland
Total miles since Bristol: 2881.9 nm

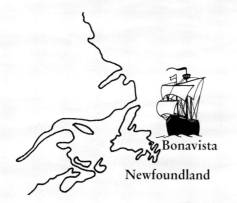

Acknowledgments

I first have to thank my family for allowing me to explore and live out my desire for adventure. They have been there for me with both financial and emotional support.

Many thanks to Maire Dalton, director of the Newfoundland and Labrador Sailing Association, without whose support sailing would not have become the major part of my life that it is today. She has given me numerous opportunities to expand my sailing horizons in Newfoundland and around the world.

Thanks to John Amatt, who encouraged me to try out for the *Matthew* crew. He also introduced me to the idea of this publishing project and to the importance of approaching everyday life with an "adventure attitude."

I am also grateful to the late Sister Mary Nolasco whose strength of heart and mind rejuvenated my soul when my low spirits were low.

Thanks to Ann Macmillan of the Canadian Broadcasting Corporation, who picked me up from a train station somewhere in Southern England and drove me to the ship. Her interest in the *Matthew* Project provided Canada with an insightful look at what makes the ship special.

The dedicated work of everyone involved with the *Matthew* Project in Bristol and the Cabot 500 Celebrations in Newfoundland contributed to the ultimate success of the voyage. Gratitude is due to the *Matthew*'s generous owner, Mike Slade, who provided the financial support which made our transatlantic crossing both exciting and safe. Thanks to everyone at the *Matthew* Project office who took care of me in Bristol, especially Georgie, Diane, Melanie, David and Colin. And to Sam Dean who literally taught me the ropes!

I was fortunate to join the 18 other members of the "Medieval Atlantic Crossing Club" to "go out and explore" as Cabot did 500 years ago. Each crew member was an invaluable part of a team which met many challenges during the adventure of a lifetime. Thanks for the experience and the memories.

Thank-you to the people of Bristol and Newfoundland and Labrador who came out to greet the *Matthew*. Your presence and energy made the adventure much more meaningful.

Finally, thank-you to Clyde Rose and everyone at Breakwater Books who saw something in the jumble of thoughts and feelings that was given to them, and particularly to Lara Maynard, the only fluent reader of my handwriting I know. Without her editing skills this book would be unreadable.

Chris LeGrow

Landlubber's Glossary

abeam: opposite the middle of the side of a ship; or, straight across a ship

aft: at or near the stern of a ship

astern: aft; toward or at the rear of a ship

belaying pin: a pin in a ship's rail around which ropes can be fastened

bilge: the lowest part of the hold of a ship; also the bottom of the hull of a ship

bonnet: a piece of canvas attached to a sail in light winds to increase the area of the sail

bosun: boatswain; a ship's officer responsible for the rigging, anchors and ropes, and directing some of the work of the crew

brail: a small rope used in drawing a sail in or up

broach: to turn broadside on to the sea and wind

bulwarks: the side of the ship which extends like a fence above its deck

castle: a high structure on the deck of early ships

clew: a corner on a square sail or fore-and-aft sail; or a metal ring fastened on such a corner to allow the attachment of lines

crow's nest: a lookout platform near the top of the mast of a ship

drabbler: a piece of canvas which is laced to a sail to increase its depth

doldrums: ocean regions near the equator where the wind is weak or shifts constantly; sailing ships in doldrums have difficulty making any headway

fo'c'sle: forecastle; the upper deck in front of the foremast of a ship

forecourse: foresail; the square sail attached to the lowest yard of a ship's forward mast

foredeck: the part of a ship's main deck closest to the bow

foresail: see forecourse

forestay: a cable or rope extending from a ship's foremast to its bowsprit

forestay sail: the first sail in front of a ship's forward mast; it is a triangular sail attached to the forestay

galley: a ship's kitchen

growlers: pieces of floating ice which have broken off an iceberg

half-ton spar: a stout pole used to support a ship's vessel

halyard: a tackle or rope used to lower or raise a ship's flag, yard or sail

head: the lavatory of a ship

helm: the wheel or handle used to steer a ship

Jacob's ladder: a ladder made of rope with metal or wooden rungs used on ships

jury-rig: a temporary rig on a ship

lateen sail: a triangular sail on a short mast which is held up by a long yard

mainsail: the largest sail of a ship; it is located on the mainmast or principal mast of a ship

mainstay: a rope or wire supporting the mainmast of a ship and extending to the bow

manrope: a rope used as a handrail at the side of a ship's ladder or gangway

mizzen: mizzenmast; the mast closest to the stern of a two- or three-masted sailing vessel; or, the fore-and-aft sail on the mizzenmast

mooring lines: lines used to secure or tie up a ship

nav room: the navigation room on a ship

nm: nautical mile; a sea mile, the standard unit of nautical distance is the equivalent of 6 076.11549 feet

palm: a leather pad with a metal plate in the center worn over the palm of the hand and used much like a thimble when sewing sails or related items

poop deck: the deck at the stern of the ship; it often forms the cabin's roof

rail: the upper part of a ship's bulwarks

ratlines: small ropes that cross the shrouds of a ship; they are used for going aloft

rib: a curved member of the frame of a ship which goes out from the keel

rigger: a person who rigs a ship, fitting it with masts, sails and ropes

rigging: the chains, cables and ropes used to work and support a ship's masts, sails and yards

shrouds: a series of ropes that help support a ship's mast

spar: a stout pole used to support a ship's vessel

sprit: a pole reaching diagonally from the top corner of a foot-and-aft sail to the foot of a mast; it supports the sail

spritsail: a foot-and-aft sail supported by a sprit

starboard: the right side of a ship when facing forward

struck: lowered

tallow: to coat with a greasy substance

tack: a zigzag course against the wind; or, the direction of a ship's movement in regard to the position of its sails and wind direction

tar: to cover with tar; a ship's masts may be tarred to prevent the wood from rotting

tiller: a handle at the stern of a ship used to turn its rudder

yard: a long, slender beam or pole fastened across a mast and used to support a sail